FIELD ROAST

101 ARTISAN VEGAN MEAT RECIPES TO COOK, SHARE & SAVOR

FIELD ROAST

Tommy McDonald

Da Capo
LIFE
LONG

Editorial production by Christine Marra, Marrathon Production Services. www.marrathoneditorial.org

Designed by Lisa Diercks, Endpaper Studio. www.endpaperstudio.com

Set in FF Quixo and Veneer

Cataloging-in-Publication data for this book is available from the Library of Congress.

First Da Capo Press edition 2017
ISBN: 978-0-7382-1959-2 (hardcover)
ISBN: 978-0-7382-1980-6 (e-book)

Published by Da Capo Press, an imprint of Perseus Books, LLC, a subsidiary of Hachette Book Group, Inc. www.dacapopress.com

Printed in Canada

FRI
10 9 8 7 6 5 4 3 2 1

To the generations of foodmakers who have come before us, thank you for your skills, techniques and bold explorations. Your struggles and inspirations give us life today! This book is dedicated to you.

CONTENTS

FOREWORD

Twenty years ago, while developing a vegan teriyaki wrap for a friend's business in Seattle, I stumbled upon the concept that would later become Field Roast vegetarian grain meats. My friend was starting an artisan bakery: hand forming loaves of bread, carefully crafting them into something beautiful and delicious. I was searching for a vegan protein food for a sandwich wrap that would provide satisfaction; tofu was too soft and the fake meat substitutes lacked honesty and were overly processed. Inspiration! Why not create an artisan-crafted, authentically flavored, real vegetarian meat—like an artisan loaf of bread, except for vegan meat? I discovered the centuries-old Asian tradition of using wheat as a protein food, such as *mien ching* (Buddha's food) or seitan. I was amazed—such great mouthfeel and tooth resistance. All that was missing were bold flavors and the right physical shapes—sausages, roasts, and loaves. Inspired by the traditional European heritage of the artisan breads my friend was making, I found the European charcuterie tradition of sausage, pâté, and meat making. I combined the foods from two continents and a company was born: the Field Roast Grain Meat Company, a blend of European and Asian heritage. This book, carefully crafted and written by Field Roast executive chef Tommy McDonald, brings to light for the very first time the tips and techniques we use to make our Field Roast brand vegetarian grain meats. In the last two decades, Seattle has witnessed a culinary renaissance not only in the high-end restaurant world but also as a result of the region's amazing multicultural makeup . . . Asian, African and Latin American cultures. Tommy's food skills reflect the next generation of chefs who have come of age during this renaissance and take our rich multicultural food world as a matter of course. The recipes in this cookbook reflect Tommy's

Seattle roots and the dynamic culinary environment he has emerged from.

At the Field Roast Grain Meat Company, our goal is to make the best veggie sausages, roasts, and deli slices we possibly can—using the multitude of plant-based ingredients and flavors that abound. Without being bound to imitate the flavor and sinew of animal meat, we have been able to create foods that taste good on their own merit, utilizing the same ingredients that we title our product flavors—"Smoked Apple Sage," "Wild Mushroom," and "Smoked Tomato," to

PEPPER-STUFFED
BURGERS, PAGE 49

name a few. Sometimes the simplest of ideas have great impact and merit.

At Field Roast our first step has always been to create a right environment before making our foods. This means many things: giving honor to our employees as the individuals they are outside of work—fathers, sons, mothers, daughters, artists, athletes, immigrants, musicians, and so on. It means gathering together as a company for our monthly community meeting where we hear from one another, celebrate our anniversaries and milestones, and discuss struggles and improvement needs. It means creating a physical environment of beauty and openness, installing windows into our production areas—letting the sunlight in, keeping our facilities well maintained, cultivating a community garden outside in our parking lot. These are the subtle yet important elements that make our products attractive and our customers happy.

Our customers want to know who is making their food, how their food is being made, and where their food is made. We often give tours at our Seattle plant, showing our customers and friends how Field Roast is made. This is unique in an industry that can often be secretive and oblique. In this book, we've gone one step further and have shared some of our basic techniques in recipe form. Soon you will be making your own vegan sausages, stuffed roasts, and meatloaf just as we do. This makes us very happy because every pound of vegan meat made means one pound less of animal meat consumed. This is better for our health, our community, and our planet.

At the end of 2016, Field Roast celebrated its twentieth year in business. What a difference twenty years makes—I have seen vegan foods go from highly niched and regularly disparaged as tasteless and fake to generally accepted, popular with politicians and celebrities, and most definitely mainstream. Today we sell Field Roast not only to natural foods stores and restaurants but also Walmart, Costco, Kroger, and most of the major league baseball and football stadiums across the country. Some time ago it became obvious that it was time to hang up my chef's jacket and pass the baton. I quickly discovered a new generation of foodmakers, a generation that takes vegan foods for granted without being combative partisans, and is comfortable with not only traditional American foods but also the emerging culture cuisines of our times. I'm confident that you will find the enclosed collection of recipes delicious and enjoyed by all the "vores" in your community: carnivores, omnivores, and veggievores.

—*David Lee, Field Roast founder and president*

KHAO SOI, PAGE 84

PANZANELLA SKEWERS, PAGE 151

INTRODUCTION: WE LOVE MEAT

WHEN I FIRST started working at Field Roast, we all had the same black T-shirt with the Field Roast logo on the front and the Merriam-Webster definition of the word *meat* on the back:

A: food; especially: solid food as distinguished from drink

B: the edible part of something as distinguished from its covering (as a husk or shell)

C: the part of something that can be eaten

D: the most important part

I realize that when most people hear the word *meat*, they think of the part of their meal that comes from an animal—and so, the idea of grain meat may initially seem odd. But hang tight: we're onto something here. In crafting delicious meat from grains, we're following in the footsteps of ancient culinary traditions that have been using grains as a staple in their diet for thousands of years. And for good reason: the outstanding nutritional properties and high protein content can't be ignored.

For us, grains are the center of the plate and are the foundation of our sausages, burgers, and roasts. The process is simple and time-honored, and the ingredients are immune to fads or trends. In much the way that we've broadened our understanding of the word *milk* to include soy and nut milks, at Field Roast we're excited about doing the same for meat. Because when you remove animal protein from your meals, you're not left with an absence or a gap, you're left with the opportunity to broaden your understanding of what meat is and what center-of-the-plate food can be.

SIMPLY MADE FROM GRAINS, VEGETABLES, AND LEGUMES

One thing that excited me about Field Roast products from the very beginning is their simplicity. When I'm shopping for food, point of origin is a major consideration: Where did the product come from? Where was it made? What is it made from? When I think of most vegetarian meat products, this is pretty hard to imagine. Grain meat is different: we start with a simple wheat flour, so it's easy to envision what it's made from and where it began. It's a process that can be done in the comfort of your own kitchen without industrial machines and without gums and binders, and one that I'm really looking forward to sharing with you.

Plants Drive Flavor

When you hear the word vegan, what comes to mind? A militant lifestyle rife with kale, tahini, and social justice? You may imagine a pale, scrawny co-op employee enrobed in irony, and perhaps some polyester brown slacks fresh from the Goodwill. But the landscape is shifting, and now we talk about new ideas, bold flavors, clean eating, and good food! Eating vegan, or plant-based, doesn't require you to change everything about yourself. It could be a couple of weeks a month, a couple of days a week, even a few meals here and there, or it could be every waking moment. Regardless of how often you are eating vegan, now is a wonderful time to do it.

My style of cooking and our philosophy at Field Roast is a departure from a lot of the vegan products and recipes you may already know. Rather than trying to mimic the flavor and texture of animal products, we craft recipes that set out to re-create the spirit of the dish, while showcasing the flavors of the plants it is made from. In other words, why work tirelessly to make a vegan sausage that tastes like pork when you could make one that tastes like what it's actually made from: peppers, apples, and grains?

FIELD ROAST FOOD TRADITIONS— A COMBINATION OF EUROPEAN AND ASIAN HERITAGE

A New, Old Idea

Grain meat has a rich culinary heritage beginning in China, when Buddhist monks created a method to produce a high-protein dough made from wheat that they called *mien ching*. What the monks found was that if you took a simple wheat flour dough, submerged it in a bowl of water, and kneaded it thoroughly, a physical change would begin to occur. The starches from the dough would begin to fall away, turning the water a milky white color and creating a firm and elastic dough. That process of washing the wheat made a dough that could contain up to 80 percent pure protein. At this point, the monks would steam or boil the dough, slice it, and cook it with sea vegetables, mushrooms, ginger, and broth. When Buddhism began its migration to other countries, the idea of this revolutionary grain meat traveled from China to Japan, where it became known under many different names and today is known as seitan.

This idea remained in the east until the 1800s, when Chinese and Japanese immigrants brought many of their traditional foods with them, including *mien ching* and seitan—and the process made its way through Europe and into the United States. The growth in popularity of seitan was slow, much of it remaining largely unknown to the broader culture until the natural foods movement of the 1970s.

A Collision of Culinary Traditions

Chef David Lee spent a time working with different kinds of vegetarian proteins and their application in everyday meals. Seitan and meat made from grains stuck out to him as a great satiating, center-of-the-plate choice that could serve as a vehicle for bold flavor. This grain meat had the makings of a food with the texture and tooth resistance needed for sausages, deli sandwiches, burgers, and roasts. David began tweaking and experimenting with the process, eventually incorporating many classic techniques essential to making charcuterie into his process. David found himself continuing to think about joining these two traditions—the ancient practice of making grain meat and the French culinary tradition of charcuterie—and the possibilities to create a brand new product felt endless. As the product improved, he began working it in to different food design products he was doing for local food makers and the product started to gain some buzz. With a growing demand, David continued to experiment with new ideas and started churning out exciting new products, and with that, Field Roast was born.

A New Paradigm of Real Vegan Meat Is Born

The Field Roast Grain Meat Company was founded in 1997 by David Lee and his brother Richard out of a real desire to see a different vegetarian product on store shelves. So many of the vegetarian protein products available then were made with soy and difficult-to-pronounce ingredients, or relied on dehydrated or previously frozen foods. So, they worked to bring their vegetarian loaves—made with grains, vegetables, and spices—to market, and found a home for them at a local Seattle co-op called PCC Natural Markets. The loaves took off and began popping up in national grocery chains.

As with most small businesses, it wasn't easy growth—there were lots of kinks to work out, investors to sign on, and staff to streamline, but the late hours and determination started to pay off. Customers were excited to have a vegan option with ingredients you could feel good about eating.

In 2005, Field Roast launched its line of sausages—a big step for the company, as the other vegan sausages on the market were emulsified and spongy. But Field Roast used an entirely new method, working with the wheat grind, binding it, and tying it off using a classic charcuterie technique. These sausages were juicy and toothsome and appealed to a broader audience of grocery shoppers. Finally, Field Roast was catapulted into the mainstream and cemented as a leader in the vegan meat sector. Today, you can find Field Roast's high-protein vegan meats and cheeses at a number of national grocery stores—everything from sausages to stuffed roasts, deli slices, frankfurters, FieldBurgers, and vegan Chao Cheese Slices. David is as closely involved today as he was in the 1990s, and Field Roast is even more of a family business with his sons Malcolm and Ian having hopped on board.

SEATTLE'S INFLUENCE AND MY APPROACH: KNOW YOUR FOOD

The Early Days

On a rainy day in November 1851, Arthur Denny landed at Alki Point with a group of family and friends. He was met at the shore by his brother David, who had traveled ahead of the group to scout out a place for a new settlement in the Pacific Northwest. David had spent the fall in a roofless cabin on Puget Sound, and was so defeated by the time the party reached the beach at Alki that the only greeting he could muster was, "I wish you hadn't come."

In Seattle we call that SAD (seasonal affective disorder), and it *is* real. One winter it rained for thirty-three days in a row: that's enough to dampen anyone's pioneering spirit. But what the Denny party learned, besides the fact that you should probably put a roof on your cabin, was that once May rolled around and the rain stopped, things were actually pretty nice in their little seaside village.

Since those early days, Seattle has seen periods of immense growth, providing the timber to build many West Coast cities in the 1800s, holding firm as a supply port for the Alaskan gold rush, and attracting innovators and industry pioneers to work for such companies as Microsoft, Boeing, Starbucks, and Amazon. Trade has driven Seattle's growth, and has attracted people of all ethnicities and cultures to experience, work, and raise families here. And of course that means a rich diversity of music, history, art, and food.

Growing Up in the PNW

I was born in Seattle in 1986 to a big, loving, and loud family. The best kind. Both my parents worked when I was a kid, so my siblings and I were always expected to help out around the house, and prepare our own meals. During the summers this was especially important as we had all those extra hours around the house that were usually spent at school. We did a pretty good job of keeping ourselves busy, and it was always made much easier when I was sent off to work out at "the Ranch," my granny's house.

Granny lives in the tiny town of Joyce, Washington, famous (to us) for their wild blackberries and idyllic summers. Joyce skirts up to the

MAKING HARVEST HOLIDAY ROAST, PAGE 20

Strait of Juan de Fuca, a waterway that separates Washington State from Vancouver Island. During my summers there, I helped care for all the animals (cows, chickens, pigs, rabbits, cats, a goat named Fart, a duck, and her dogs), and learned how to clear brush, haul hay, and split and stack firewood.

It was during those summers that I learned to love food, largely because I'd played such a big part in growing and harvesting it. At the Ranch, I'd learned how to barbecue on a rusted-out steel drum welded onto a crank arm–adorned frame (the grill of a lifetime). We grilled everything during the summer because it was just "too dang hot to turn on the oven," according to Granny. Once I was old enough to get a real job, I started working in kitchens, trying to save money for college. I bounced around to kitchens big and small, clean and dirty, busy and really busy. As I learned more, I also learned how much I already knew: that making good food was about understanding everything that went into it.

Today I think back to the Seattle of my youth and the experiences that have brought me to where I am today—and a lot has changed. Seattle is definitely more of an urban metropolis than it was decades ago. And I have to say, a lot of my friends who live here or in other cities around the country tend to favor convenience over anything when it comes to cooking meals at home or feeding themselves. I get that; we all lead busy lives. But I think we can strive to have a better relationship with our food. It could be as small as watering a potted basil plant on your windowsill. Or it could be simply asking some questions or doing a little research on an ingredient you're not familiar with next time you're eating out or traveling. Vegan or not, knowing what we're putting on our plate

(and in our body) and where it comes from has become my passion. I hope a little of it rubs off on you, too.

The Recipes: Make Them Your Own

So many recipes set off in one direction and, after I've made them a number of times, they end up looking completely different. I'm sure the same is true for you. Don't like asparagus? Swap in broccoli or zucchini. Out of wild rice? Brown rice will do just fine. Cooking is fluid and, to be honest, I think it's more fun when we take recipes and make them our own, so please feel free to make swaps and tweaks based on your tastes and preferences. You'll notice in many of the recipes here we suggest our Field Roast brand products, which you can either make at home using the methods I lay out here or buy at your favorite grocery store.

Vegan Meat Is for Everyone!

Eating a vegan meal and maintaining a vegan diet are two completely different things. And while this is most certainly a vegan cookbook, this book was written for everyone. Throughout these pages, you're going to find flavor-packed, plant-based recipes that I hope will become new favorites—food you'll want to share with family, friends, and co-workers. You'll find some of my favorite comfort foods, including vegan macaroni and cheese, stuffed burgers, and ranch potatoes, but you'll also find more refined favorites, such as chilled asparagus salad and white bean and eggplant crostini. There are more involved recipes where we'll actually teach you how to make our grain meat, but there are dozens and dozens of simple, fuss-free recipes you can pull together on an average weeknight, too. So, really: there's something for everyone here. Vegan or not, let's dig in.

ESSENTIAL INGREDIENTS & TOOLS OF OUR TRADE

ALTHOUGH WE make Field Roast products on a large scale at our Seattle headquarters, you don't need fancy equipment or machinery to get the same results at home. Here's a guide to the most helpful pieces of kitchen equipment to tackle the recipes in this book—it's not meant to be exhaustive, but more a call-out to some of the most-used and more essential tools of our trade. Let's do this.

BAMBOO STEAMER BASKETS These come in many sizes and are stackable, so they are great for steaming lots of sausages at once. All you need is a set of two or three and a large pot to set them on. Start with 2 quarts of water at a gentle boil, and add a pint of water every 30 to 40 minutes. I also use these to steam my stuffed roasts, I have a 14-inch basket that I bought at the Asian supermarket down the street from my house for pretty cheap, and these roast recipes should fit perfectly.

BUTCHER'S TWINE For tying off roasts and sausages, and countless other kitchen needs. This can be found at most grocery stores or kitchen supply stores. I buy mine in a big spool from the restaurant supply store.

CHEESECLOTH For wrapping the roasts and our meat grinds, cheesecloth is essential. You can find it at any well-stocked kitchen store, or online at a specialty grocery retailer (see Sources, page 211).

DUTCH OVEN OR LARGE POT For a few of the recipes in this book, you'll need a large, heavy-bottomed pot. I reach for my Dutch oven at home, but any large pot should do the trick.

FOOD PROCESSOR To make our meat grind, the jumping-off point for many of the recipes in this book, you're going to need a food processor. At Field Roast, we actually use a meat grinder, but in a pinch you can get great results with a run-of-the-mill food processor instead. We also use the food processor as a shortcut for making piecrusts and minced vegetables.

HIGH-SPEED BLENDER A high-speed blender, such as a Vitamix, is so helpful in blending up dressings and sauces, and while I generally hate clutter on the countertops, this is one exception I make at home. They aren't cheap, but in my opinion, the machine is worth every penny—and will last for years.

MEAT GRINDER There are many different types of meat grinders, but the one I use attaches right to my KitchenAid stand mixer. You can find these online, or at a well-appointed kitchen shop. This attachment will also double as a sausage stuffer with the right "sausage horn" attachment.

SALAD SPINNER I use a lot of seasonal vegetables and fresh herbs in my cooking, and my favorite way to quickly wash and prep them is with a basic salad spinner.

SAUSAGE CASING Most sausage casings available are made using animal parts, which won't work for us. LEM Products makes plastic hotdog casings (26 mm) that fit perfectly on to the sausage horn attachment for the KitchenAid stand mixer. These are durable and easy to use, and can be ordered from LEM Products directly (see Sources, page 211) or even Amazon.

SAUSAGE STUFFER OR SAUSAGE STUFFER ATTACHMENT Unless you're making a lot of sausage at home, chances are a sausage stuffer isn't hanging out in your cupboards. If you have a KitchenAid stand mixer at home, the good news is the company makes a great attachment that works as a grinder and a sausage stuffer. Sometimes you can find them online as a kit; otherwise you may have to buy the "sausage horn" separate from the grinder.

THERMOMETER An instant-read thermometer takes a lot of the guesswork out of cooking—something I'm always grateful for.

UTENSILS AND SUCH Every well-stocked kitchen should have a *good whisk*, a *chef's knife* with an 8- to 10-inch blade, and a *paring knife* with a 4- to 5-inch blade. A few stainless-steel or wooden *spoons* are great for stirring, and *stainless-steel tongs* are essential for cooking on the stovetop or for pulling hot food off the grill. The *Microplane* is my go-to for zesting fresh citrus, and while not completely necessary, a *mandoline* is great for making thinly sliced vegetables quickly and uniformly for salads and slaws.

THE FIELD ROAST PANTRY

Many of the ingredients in this book are things you may already have at home or, at the very least, can easily find at your neighborhood grocery store. But there are a few that may be less familiar, so I wanted to take a minute to run them by you so we're all on the same page.

Everyday Staples

We always have the following ingredients on hand to make our meat grind, sausages, roasts, and burgers. In that way, they're essential pantry ingredients around here—as critical to us as flour and sugar are to a seasoned baker.

GARBANZO FLOUR A pulse flour made from ground chickpeas, also known as gram flour. We use this in our roast recipes to add tenderness and soften the bite of the strong high gluten flour. You can find garbanzo flour in most natural grocery stores and Whole Foods Market; it's also available online.

VEGAN BEEF, CHICKEN, AND VEGETABLE BASE These vegan bases are highly concentrated flavored pastes that come from reducing stock until almost all the liquid is gone. Most natural foods stores offer vegan versions of chicken and beef flavors, which are a blend of plant flavors meant to closely resemble the same profile. We use these bases in these recipes to add rich plant flavors to our meats.

VITAL WHEAT GLUTEN Vital wheat gluten is one of the core ingredients of our meats. It is a very high protein flour from wheat. This is the product of the "washing the dough" process. Essentially this is wheat flour with the carbohydrates (starches) washed away. You can find vital wheat gluten in most natural grocery stores, Whole Foods Market, and also online.

Vegan Dairy

COCONUT CREAM Coconut cream is much richer than coconut milk. It can be purchased at most grocery stores, especially specialty grocers and Asian markets. The cream that rises to the top of a can of coconut milk is also considered coconut cream.

PLANT-BASED MILKS When you see a recipe calling for plant-based milks, feel free to use your favorite—I usually reach for almond, but any nut, soy, or alternative milk will work just fine, just make sure they are unflavored and unsweetened.

VEGAN BUTTER I always have vegan butter on hand to use in everything from fluffy biscuits to silky sauces. For a long time I used only Earth Balance Buttery Spread, which has a low melting point, more like margarine, and has a buttery flavor. Recently I have started to see vegan butters with a higher melting point that more closely resemble butter. Miyoko's Creamery makes a delicious cultured product that you can find in most natural foods stores, and also online. The recipes in this book ask for both, but can be interchanged depending on preference or availability.

VEGAN CREAM CHEESE Cream cheese comes up in a lot of our recipes, and I can't recommend Kite Hill brand enough (available nationwide). It's a naturally cultured product made from delicious and expertly crafted almond milk.

VEGAN EGGS I rely on two vegan egg products in the kitchen, and they both play a different role. First up is Vegg, which comes in a powder that you mix up to make an actual egg yolk. Imagine a runny vegan egg yolk to use on top of salads, benedicts, and stirred into sauces. Vegg relies on black salt and nutritional yeast, which gives it that characteristic egg flavor and color. If you have trouble finding it, you can use equal parts nutritional yeast instead. Second, I can't live without Follow Your Heart vegan eggs, which you can mix up to be more of a full egg to use when you're looking for both the yolk and the white—or to make killer scrambled eggs. You can use other powdered egg substitutes in a pinch, but I have found that the Follow Your Heart vegan egg has some unique properties that make for great flavor and texture.

VEGAN MAYO I like Just Mayo brand better than most vegan mayos because it doesn't separate when you add it to something hot, so it's great to cook with—and readily available at most grocery stores.

FROM THE FIELDS

Throughout these pages you'll see regional ingredients getting a lot of play: apples and pears, hearty greens such as kale and arugula, beets, fennel, and mushrooms (especially chanterelle, oyster, and trumpet). Cooking with local ingredients whenever possible just ensures they're fresher as they haven't had to travel as far, and here in Seattle we're lucky to have a few great year-round farmers' markets that make the hunt, so to speak, pretty easy. The following are a few fresh ingredients that are, sadly, not local and may not be as familiar in your home kitchen.

JACKFRUIT This is a large, spiky tree fruit common in Southeast Asian cooking, which you can find canned in Asian markets or well-stocked grocery stores. We use young jackfruit in our recipes. While jackfruit typically has a sweet flavor, when it's young it's more firm and much less sweet, and when it's cooked down, it shreds easily like carnitas or brisket, so it's a great plant-based center-of-the-plate option.

KIMCHI In general, *kimchi* refers to any fermented vegetable, but napa cabbage is definitely the most common inclusion in this colorful Korean side condiment. Thanks to its recent popularity, kimchi is now really easy to find at a well-stocked grocery store or Asian food market.

KOMBU A member of the kelp family, kombu brings immense umami flavor to everything it touches. Look for it dried and packaged in Asian food markets or well-stocked grocery stores. See page 19 for a more in-depth look.

ROASTED SUGAR PIE
PUMPKIN STEW, PAGE 95

LEMONGRASS Lemongrass is widely used in Asian cuisines, and can be purchased dried or fresh—I prefer the latter. It used to be tricky to find, but now many mainstream grocery stores have it proudly displayed in the vegetable aisle. If you've never worked with it in the kitchen, lemongrass has a mild citrus flavor and brings a really special brightness to savory dishes, such as salads, soups, and stews. When shopping for lemongrass, do know that the majority of its flavor resides in the lower stalks, which is why many stores sell it this way, choosing to cut away its leafy tops. In the kitchen, you can use it in one of two ways: break it up and use it whole—much like a bay leaf—to flavor stocks and soups. To do this, turn your chef's knife over and pound the lemongrass to break open the membranes and help release the flavor. I'll even cover it with a towel and give it a good roll on my cutting board—just be mindful that you want the stalk to remain intact so it's easy to remove from your dish before serving. Alternatively, you can peel off the outer layers and mince the lemongrass finely, adding it to marinades, salad dressings, and curry pastes for flavor. Store it in an airtight container or wrap in plastic wrap, refrigerated, for up to three weeks.

LIQUID SMOKE A superconcentrated seasoning. I use liquid smoke sparingly to get that warm, smoky flavor into foods without the lengthy smoking process. Most well-stocked grocery stores should have it.

MEYER LEMONS I occasionally get specific with my citrus and call for Meyer lemons—not to be fussy, but because they really are sweeter and their rind is more fragrant and less astringent than a regular lemon.

MIRIN A type of seasoned rice wine common in Japanese cooking (and a core ingredient in teriyaki sauce), mirin lends a sweet acidity to a recipe—making it a fitting contrast for saltier flavors, such as soy or tamari. Asian food markets and most well-stocked grocery stores should have it available.

MISO Miso is made from fermented soybeans and comes in a few different colors ranging from white to dark red. Earthy, salty and pungent, miso is an essential seasoning for sauces and marinades as well as meats and vegetables. Miso is available at Asian markets and well-stocked grocery stores.

NATURAL SUGARS You'll notice that the recipes in this book rely on natural sweeteners, such as agave syrup, coconut sugar, and date sugar, instead of granulated sugar. Because they're minimally processed, natural sweeteners often contain nutrients that no longer exist in refined white sugars and therefore are thought to be a healthier choice. In addition to the possibility of a more nutritious sweetener, I'm really drawn to natural sugars because they each have distinct flavors that make them interesting and exciting to experiment with in the kitchen. Agave is light and quite sweet, whereas coconut sugar has a dark, almost damp sweetness, and date sugar is subtle and caramelly.

NUTRITIONAL YEAST If you've ever made a tofu scramble (or hang out with people who do), you probably know nutritional yeast. This dairy-free, savory seasoning has an addictive cheesy, nutty flavor that's great in sauces, casseroles, and bakes, and sprinkled on top of salads, soups, or popcorn. You can find nutritional yeast in natural grocery stores, Whole Foods market, and online.

SPICES & SEASONINGS To ensure I'm working with the freshest spices possible, I often grind them myself or, at the very least, buy them in bulk (you never know how long those little glass jars have been sitting on the shelves). As for herbs, there's nothing like fresh herbs to bring color, fragrance, and flavor to a dish. I know it can sometimes feel like an extra ingredient to add to the shopping list, but I'm a firm believer that buying herbs fresh makes all the difference. If you'd rather use dried herbs, a good rule of thumb is to substitute dried herbs for fresh at a ratio of 1:3 (so if your recipe calls for 1 tablespoon of fresh oregano, you'd want to use 1 teaspoon of dried instead).

TAMARI & SHOYU You may often hear tamari and soy sauce talked about in the same sentence, and while similar at the outset, tamari has a darker color and richer flavor than soy sauce and is usually made with little to no wheat. Shoyu, on the other hand, is a little different: it has a more full-bodied flavor and is considered a living food with probiotic qualities. I buy mine at the natural foods store, but I realize this is an ingredient that may be tough to find, so feel free to use a tamari or soy sauce if you have trouble tracking it down.

MAKING VEGAN CHARCUTERIE AT HOME

GETTING STARTED

IN THE FIELD ROAST KITCHEN, we're not trying to replicate animal-based sausages, roasts, or pâté. So, making a vegetarian product that tastes and reminds you of chicken or pork isn't really our thing. Instead, what really excites us is focusing on the incredible plant-based flavors at the ready with vegetables, herbs, and spices. And the addition of wheat gives each of our recipes that characteristic "meaty" texture while also imparting a good bit of protein. Making vegan charcuterie isn't difficult and our technique uses simple ingredients that you'll be able to find at your favorite grocery store. Let's get started!

5 TIPS TO MAKING GREAT SAUSAGE AT HOME

Buying sausage at the store is certainly convenient, but making your own is supergratifying and you get the bonus of getting to choose exactly which flavors you'd like to feature. If you're new to making sausage, here are a few quick tips to set you up for success right out of the gate:

1. Consider your workspace. Clear off your counters so they're clutter-free, set up your equipment, and make sure to read the recipe all the way through so you have everything you need. The process is simple, but it does require a little space.

2. You'll need casing to contain your meat grind into a sausage shape. If you have trouble finding casing, use a rectangle of waxed paper and some foil instead. Spray the waxed paper with oil, and form some dough into a sausage shape. Using the waxed paper, roll the dough like a cigar, making sure it's evenly distributed throughout. Fold the ends of the paper inward to seal them off, and roll the foil around the outside to hold it all in place. Fold the ends of the foil up to seal them off—and now your sausage is all set for steaming.

3. Don't try to cook too many sausages at once. You want to make sure your sausages have enough space to cook evenly and thoroughly, so avoid the temptation to save time. Cook them in batches instead.

4. Think ahead: while you're at it, why not make some extras for the freezer? Store them in an airtight freezer bag, and they'll keep for up to six months. You can also double your grind recipe and freeze it for future impromptu sausage-making.

5. Have fun and improvise. The first time you do something new in the kitchen, chances are you follow the recipe pretty closely. But after you become comfortable with the process, feel free to swap out vegetables and spices to create seasonal options that you really love. The possibilities are endless.

5 TIPS TO MAKING GREAT ROASTS AT HOME

Making roasts at home requires less equipment than making sausage, and is a great first foray into making plant-based meat. If you've never tied a roast before, don't worry—I'll walk you through it. Allow yourself enough time so you don't feel rushed and make sure you have a nice, clear workspace. Beyond that, here are a few tips to ensure your roasts are as tasty as ours:

1. When you're mixing the meat together, there may be some excess liquid that is not absorbed by the dry ingredients. This is common and not a problem at all: you'll want to just discard it at the very end.

2. The meat of the roast is going to be tough and elastic. Don't worry if it doesn't look perfect at first; once you get it wrapped and tied up, it will really start to look like a roast.

3. Make sure you spray your cheesecloth with oil (we use either sunflower, safflower, or canola) to ensure that it doesn't stick to the roast.

4. Be sure not to tie the roast too tightly. The twine should be taut, but not cinched so tight that it creates ribs in the meat.

5. Don't stress about your knots: If you're not familiar with a butcher's slipknot, use any simple slip-knot, and space them every inch or so. A slipknot is created by making a P-shaped loop at one end of the string, then taking hold of the other end of the string and bringing it through the loop. Using the same end of the string, next make a knot around the P-shaped loop and pull tight on the opposite end to set it.

ROASTS, STUFFED ROASTS, BREADED CUTLETS

LEMONGRASS AND GINGER ROAST

 **MAKES 1 ROAST, ABOUT 8 SERVINGS**

A T FIELD ROAST, WE USE our roasts in more ways than I can count: chopped up in salads, breaded for cutlets, or thinly sliced in deluxe deli sandwiches. This recipe makes a roast that's light and bright in flavor, made with our Lemongrass and Ginger Stock (page 195), tender leeks and green onion, and fragrant garlic. Although it's certainly great any time of year, it always reminds me of spring and seems most fitting in sandwiches with lots of fresh, crunchy vegetables, lighter salads, and colorful, seasonal soups. It's also great to keep on hand in the fridge for those evenings when you just can't figure out what to do for dinner as, let's face it: sandwiches are often the answer. Please note that our roast recipes do require some special equipment and cooking instructions, which you can learn more about in Making Great Roasts at Home (page 14).

DRY MIXTURE

2⅓ cups vital wheat gluten

¼ cup garbanzo flour

VEGETABLES

¼ cup coconut oil

2 leeks, cleaned and thinly sliced

3 stalks lemongrass, pounded with the back of a chef's knife (see page 9)

1 (1-inch) piece fresh ginger, peeled and minced

6 cloves garlic, minced

1 bunch green onions, thinly sliced all the way up to the root, including the white portion

2 tablespoons vegan chicken base

2 teaspoons sea salt

2 teaspoons ground coriander

LIQUID INGREDIENTS

1¾ cups Lemongrass and Ginger Stock (page 195), cold

¼ cup sake or mirin

¼ cup tamari or soy sauce

1 tablespoon sesame oil

COOKING LIQUID

4 quarts water

1½ tablespoons sea salt

RUB

2 teaspoons Chinese five-spice powder

2 teaspoons freshly ground black pepper

1 teaspoon dried ginger

2 teaspoons smoked paprika

EQUIPMENT

1 (24 x 18-inch) piece cheesecloth, folded in half to make a 12 x 18-inch piece

Safflower or canola oil spray

48 inches butcher's twine

1. Whisk the dry ingredients together in a large bowl and set aside.

2. In a skillet over medium heat, heat the coconut oil and add all the vegetable ingredients. Sauté for 20 minutes, stirring occasionally. Remove from the heat, discard the lemongrass, and cool in the fridge.

3. Combine the liquid ingredients in a large bowl and add the cooled vegetable mixture; mix together. Pour the liquid into the bowl of dry ingredients and stir together with a large spoon, then knead it lightly with your hands. The dough will be soft.

4. Combine the water and salt in a large stockpot and bring the cooking liquid to a boil.

5. Lay out the cheesecloth on a clean board and spray with oil. Form the dough into a roast shape and place it on one end of the cheesecloth. Roll up the roast in the cheesecloth, keeping it roast shaped. Cut two pieces of twine, one about 10 inches long, the other 18 inches. Twist one end of the cheesecloth to make it tight against the roast, and using the 10-inch piece of string, tie this off with a double knot. Push in the roast on the untied end, and twist the cheesecloth until the roast is snug. Tie this off, using the 18-inch piece of string, with a double knot, tying off a loop at the end to use as a handle. Tie the roast with the remaining 20 inches of string at four equidistant intervals down the roast, using a slipknot (see How to Tie a Roast photos, page 15). Holding the tied end of the roast, gently lower it into the boiling water, adjusting the heat to keep the water at an aggressive simmer. Cover and simmer for 1½ hours, or until internally it reads 180°F on an instant-read thermometer, turning over halfway through the cooking process. Remove from the liquid and allow to cool at room temperature.

6. Combine the rub spices.

7. When the roast is cool enough to handle, remove the cheesecloth and rub the roast with the spices.

8. Finish cooling the roast in the fridge, uncovered. Wrap tightly in plastic wrap when fully cooled. The roast is ready to eat, and can be sliced thin for sandwiches, roasted with vegetables, or incorporated in the recipes in this book or your own favorites.

UMAMI: CHASING BIG FLAVOR

It's said that humans have five basic tastes: sweet, salty, sour, bitter . . . and umami. So, what exactly is umami? It is described as the savory taste, or as meaty or brothy. Glutamates are the parts of food that help us taste umami. Glutamate, or glutamic acid, is a neurotransmitter that is naturally occurring in our body; it also exists in many of the foods that we eat, including mushrooms, tomatoes, and seaweed. In this book, we commonly use kombu, a dried sea vegetable used in a lot of Japanese cooking, which—when added to soups, stocks and rice—gives each a rich depth of flavor you simply can't mimic with another ingredient. We rely on kombu to intensely flavor our Mushroom and Herb Stock (page 196), which is great for darker roasts and richer flavors, as well as our Lemongrass and Ginger Stock (page 195) used to make this roast, perfect for lighter roasts and more delicate flavors. Each is distinctly and uniquely its own, although they share one important element: the unabashed celebration of umami.

HARVEST HOLIDAY ROAST

 **MAKES 6 TO 8 SERVINGS**

Tʜᴇ ᴠᴇɢᴀɴ ᴀɴsᴡᴇʀ ᴛᴏ the whole turkey, the Harvest Roast brings together our Lemongrass and Ginger Roast (page 18) and Smoked Oyster Mushroom Stuffing (page 141) for a real center-of-the-plate addition to the holiday table. While always a crowd favorite and a tabletop stunner, this one does take a bit of time and planning: you're going to form the roast, tie it off (see photo 15), and steam it before you get it in the oven to roast, so I try to tackle each of those steps the day before I'm actually serving the roast to make for a simpler, stress-free holiday.

1 batch Lemongrass and Ginger Roast dough (page 18), uncooked

1 cup Smoked Oyster Mushroom Stuffing (page 141) or stuffing recipe of choice, uncooked

¼ cup white wine

1 cup vegan vegetable stock

2 tablespoons paprika

2 cloves garlic, minced

1 tablespoon light brown sugar

2 tablespoons olive oil

3 sprigs sage

3 sprigs thyme

2 bay leaves

2 teaspoons sea salt

1 tablespoon freshly ground black pepper

1 medium-size shallot, thinly sliced

1 medium-size carrot, peeled and cut into ¾-inch chunks

2 stalks celery, cut into ½-inch chunks

1 pound red potatoes or fingerlings, cut into ½-inch chunks and rinsed

4 sprigs parsley, for garnish

EQUIPMENT

2 (24 x 18-inch) pieces cheesecloth, each folded in half to make a 12 x 18-inch piece

Safflower or canola oil spray

48 inches butcher's twine

Steamer basket

1. Prepare the Lemongrass and Ginger Roast recipe (page 18) to the end of the dough stage. Lay the cheesecloth on a clean board and spray with oil. Form the dough into a 10 x 5-inch rectangle about ¾ inch thick. Place the stuffing in the middle of the dough, and form it into a line down the middle of the 10-inch length of the dough. Bring the wide edges of the roast dough up over the filling, overlapping in the center and pinching the edge to seal well. Bring the end pieces of the roast dough up, pinching and smoothing them so they stay well sealed. It is important that you do not have any gaps or tears that expose the stuffing.

2. Cut two pieces of twine, each about 10 inches long. Twist one end of the cheesecloth to make it tight against the roast, and using one 10-inch piece of string, tie this off with a double knot. Push in the roast on the untied end, and twist the cheesecloth until the roast is snug. Tie this off, using the other

10-inch piece of string, with a double knot. Tie the roast with the remaining 18 inches of string at four equidistant intervals down the roast (see picture), using a slipknot.

3. Steam the roast in a steamer basket for 2 hours. Remove from the steamer and allow to fully cool. Remove the cheesecloth when the roast is cool enough to handle and store wrapped in plastic wrap in the fridge until ready to roast.

4. Preheat the oven to 375°F.

5. In a bowl, combine the wine, stock, paprika, garlic, brown sugar, olive oil, sage, thyme, bay leaves, salt, and pepper; whisk well. In a large roasting pan, combine the shallot, carrot, celery, and potatoes. Place the roast in the middle of the vegetables and pour the wine mixture over the top. Place the roast in the oven and cook for 1 hour 20 minutes, basting the roast every 15 minutes with the juices in the pan.

6. Carve and serve with the vegetables; garnish with parsley.

CHEF'S NOTE: *Be sure to continue basting the roast with that savory herb-flecked marinade throughout the cook time to ensure it remains nice and juicy.*

MUSHROOM AND HERB ROAST

 **MAKES 1 ROAST, ABOUT 8 SERVINGS**

A ROBUST ROAST with intense mushroom flavor, this recipe is great in hearty soups, rich stews, and your favorite deli-style sandwich. When sourcing mushrooms, look for varieties with darker, "meatier" flavor, such as morels, shiitakes, portobellos, or even cremini—and feel free to use any mixture or variety you like. The vegan beef base adds an intense, rich flavor, so if you can find it, your roast will be all the better for it. You'll notice here I've added instructions for taking your roast game to the next level with an optional herbal rub, and it's especially nice with this recipe. The contrast between the smooth, savory roast and textured black pepper edges makes for some very addictive, delicious deli meat. Please note that our roast recipes do require some special equipment and cooking instructions, which you can learn more about in Making Great Roasts at Home (page 14).

DRY INGREDIENTS

2⅓ cups vital wheat gluten

¼ cup garbanzo flour

VEGETABLES

¼ cup coconut oil

Leaves from 3 sprigs oregano

1 tablespoon tomato paste

2 shallots, sliced

¾ pound mixed fresh mushrooms, chopped

⅛ ounce dried porcini mushrooms

6 cloves garlic, minced

2 teaspoons sea salt

2 tablespoons vegan beef base

3 bay leaves

¼ cup red wine

LIQUID INGREDIENTS

1¾ cups Mushroom and Herb Stock
(page 196), cold

¼ cup red wine

¼ cup tamari or soy sauce

1 tablespoon sesame oil

COOKING LIQUID

4 quarts water

1½ tablespoons sea salt

RUB

2 teaspoons Chinese five-spice powder

2 teaspoons freshly ground black pepper

1 teaspoon dried ginger

2 teaspoons smoked paprika

EQUIPMENT

1 (24 x 18-inch) piece cheesecloth, folded in
half to make a 12 x 18-inch piece

Safflower or canola oil spray

48 inches butcher's twine

1. Whisk the dry ingredients together in a large bowl and set aside.

2. In a skillet over medium heat, heat the coconut oil and add all the vegetable ingredients, except the wine, and sauté for 20 minutes, stirring occasionally. Deglaze the pan by adding the wine and stirring with a wooden spoon, using the spoon to scrape the bits that have cooked to the pan. Reduce the liquid for 2 minutes, then remove from the heat, discard the bay leaves, and cool in the fridge.

3. Combine the liquid ingredients in a large bowl and add the cooled vegetable mixture; mix together. Pour the liquid into the bowl of dry ingredients and stir together with a large spoon, then knead lightly with your hands. The dough will be soft.

4. Combine the water and salt in a large stockpot and bring the cooking liquid to a boil.

5. Lay out the cheesecloth on a clean board and spray with oil. Form the dough into a roast shape and place it on one end of the cheesecloth. Roll up the roast in the cheesecloth, keeping it roast-shaped. Cut two pieces of twine, one about 10 inches long, the other 18 inches. Twist one end of the cheesecloth to make it tight against the roast, and using the 10-inch piece of string, tie this off with a double knot. Push in the roast on the untied end, and twist the cheesecloth until the roast is snug. Tie this off, using the 18-inch piece of string, with a double knot, tying off a loop at the end to use as a handle. Tie the roast with the remaining 20-inch piece of string at four equidistant intervals down the roast, using a slipknot (see How to Tie a Roast photos, page 15).

6. Holding the tied end of the roast, gently lower it into the boiling liquid, adjusting the heat to keep the liquid at an aggressive simmer. Cover and simmer for 1½ hours, or until internally it reads 180°F on an instant-read thermometer, turning over halfway through the cooking process. Remove from the liquid and allow to cool at room temperature.

7. Combine the rub spices.

8. When the roast is cool enough to handle, remove the cheesecloth and rub the roast with the spices.

9. Finish the cooling roast in the fridge, uncovered. Wrap tightly in plastic wrap when fully cooled. The roast is ready to eat, and can be sliced thin for sandwiches, roasted with vegetables, or incorporated in the recipes in this book or your own favorites.

STUFFING YOUR ROASTS SUCCESSFULLY

If you're making a stuffed roast, be sure to prepare the stuffing ahead of time and let it cool completely before rolling out the meat. Avoid the temptation to stuff too much into your roast or you'll have a tough time getting it closed, and make your life easy by ensuring the outer meat has completely enclosed the stuffing (no one wants to deal with burst or overflowing roasts).

STEAKHOUSE ROAST WITH VEGAN DEMI-GLACE

 **MAKES 6 SERVINGS**

WHILE THE LOCATION MAY VARY, if you want to know what I'm typically up to on New Year's Eve, it most certainly involves this Steakhouse Roast. For this special recipe, you're going to take our Mushroom and Herb Roast recipe (page 24) one step further by stuffing it with a savory vegetable blend, including mushrooms, garlic, Parmesan, and bread crumbs. I love serving this roast with our Parsnip Root Whip (page 140), but thanks to its addictive horseradish crust, the leftover slices make a great addition to your favorite sandwiches, too.

ROAST

1 batch Mushroom and Herb Roast dough (page 24)

4 medium-size dried morel mushrooms

4 cloves garlic, minced

Leaves from 4 sprigs tarragon

2 medium-size shallots, roughly chopped

1 small parsnip, peeled and roughly chopped

1 teaspoon dried rosemary

2 teaspoons sea salt

¼ cup olive oil, plus more for brushing (optional)

1 cup vegan bread crumbs

½ cup red wine

3 tablespoons horseradish, drained

3 sprigs parsley, minced

VEGAN DEMI-GLACE

4 cups Mushroom and Herb Stock (page 196)

1 tablespoon cornstarch

1 teaspoon freshly ground black pepper

GARNISH

1 tablespoon paprika

EQUIPMENT

Parchment paper

1 (24 x 18-inch) piece cheesecloth, folded in half to make a 12 x 18-inch piece

Safflower or canola oil spray

48 inches butcher's twine

Steamer basket

1. Prepare the Mushroom and Herb Roast dough as described on page 24, but do not wrap.

2. Place the dried mushrooms in a heat-safe bowl and cover with boiling water. Let sit for 3 to 4 minutes. The water will be brown and the mushrooms should be tender. Remove the mushrooms and set aside, reserving the liquid.

3. In a food processor, combine the garlic, tarragon, shallot, parsnip, rosemary, salt, mushrooms, 2 tablespoons of the reserved mushroom liquid, and 2 tablespoons of the olive oil. Pulse the mixture until it resembles a coarse tapenade. Transfer to a large mixing bowl and add ½ cup of the bread crumbs and the red wine; stir to combine.

4. Lay the cheesecloth on a clean board, fold the cheesecloth in half along the long end, and spray with oil. Form the dough into a 10 x 5-inch rectangle about ¾ inch thick. Form the vegetable mixture into a large sausage shape along the middle of the length of the dough, leaving about 1½ inches of dough margin at each end. Use only as much stuffing as will easily fit into the roast when rolled. Bring the wide edges of the roast dough up over the filling, overlapping in the center and pinching the edge to seal well. Bring the end pieces of the roast dough up, pinching and smoothing them so they stay well sealed. It is important that you do not have any gaps or tears that expose the stuffing. Roll up the roast into the cheesecloth. Cut two pieces of twine, each about 10 inches long. Twist one end of the cheesecloth to make it tight against the roast, and using one 10-inch piece of string, tie this off with a double knot. Push in the roast on the untied end, and twist the cheesecloth until the roast is snug. Tie this off, using the other 10-inch piece of string, with a double knot. Tie the roast with the remaining 20-inch piece of string at four equidistant intervals down the roast, using a slipknot (see How to Tie a Roast photos, page 15).

5. Steam the roast in a steamer basket for 2 hours. Remove from the steamer and allow to fully cool. Remove the cheesecloth when the roast is cool enough to handle and store wrapped in plastic wrap in the fridge until ready to roast.

6. In a mixing bowl, combine the remaining ½ cup of bread crumbs, the horseradish, the remaining 2 tablespoons of olive oil, and the parsley.

7. Preheat the oven to 425°F.

8. Remove the cheesecloth from the cooled roast, and brush or spray the roast with a very small amount of oil. Coat the roast with the horseradish topping, lightly pressing it to the roast to ensure it sticks.

9. Transfer the roast to a baking dish and cover. Roast in the oven for 35 minutes, remove the cover, and roast for another 15 minutes, uncovered, until the breadcrumbs begin to brown.

10. Prepare the vegan demi-glace while the roast is cooking: In a saucepan over medium heat, reduce the stock by two thirds of its volume. Lower the heat to low and add the cornstarch. Whisk until combined and simmer for another 3 to 4 minutes. Remove from the heat and stir in the pepper.

11. Remove the roast from the oven. Garnish with the paprika and serve with the demi-glace.

HOLIDAY WELLINGTON

I HAVE A HUGE IRISH CATHOLIC family and my sister's birthday is the day before Christmas Eve, so growing up we'd always start our festivities early. A big traditionalist, my mom would make beef Wellington, and while I have fond memories of the meal, I've long wanted to do a vegan version. So, this is a plant-based Wellington featuring our pâté and mushroom duxelles, all wrapped in puff pastry. You can choose either the Field Roast Classic Meatloaf or the Mushroom and Herb Roast (page 24)—the meatloaf is a little fattier and juicier, so if you want to go full-on decadent, go that route. You can use any vegan puff pastry for this recipe, which should be easy to find in the frozen foods aisle at most natural grocery stores. Just be sure to transfer it from the freezer to the fridge a few hours before you work with it to be sure it's nice and pliable.

¼ cup olive oil, plus more for brushing roast (optional)

6 cloves garlic, minced

1 medium-size shallot, minced

½ pound cremini mushrooms, cleaned with a brush or towel and sliced

2 teaspoons sea salt

Leaves from 3 sprigs thyme

Flour, for dusting

1 sheet vegan puff pastry, thawed but chilled

6 ounces Pâté de Campagne (page 46) or vegan pâté of choice

1 Mushroom and Herb Roast (page 24) or Field Roast Classic Meatloaf

2 cups Vegan Hollandaise (page 193)

Leaves from 3 sprigs tarragon, minced

1. Preheat the oven to 425°F.

2. In a skillet over medium heat, heat the oil and add the garlic and shallot. Sauté for 2 minutes, stirring occasionally. Add the mushrooms, salt, and thyme and sauté for 15 minutes, stirring occasionally. Transfer the mixture to a food processor and pulse until it resembles tapenade, return to the pan over medium heat, and cook until the liquid has been reduced and absorbed. Remove from the heat and transfer to a plate. Cool in the fridge.

3. Lay the puff pastry on a floured board, then smear the pâté in the middle, to about the length of the roast. Spoon the mushrooms on top of the pâté, and place the roast on top of that. Fold the dough over the top of the roast, then fold the opposing side over that, pressing down gently to seal. Fold each end under the roast and press lightly to seal. Transfer the roast to a baking sheet, brush with some additional oil, if desired, and bake for 45 to 55 minutes, or until the dough is lightly browned. Remove from the oven and let rest for 10 minutes.

4. While the roast is resting, heat the hollandaise in a small saucepan over medium heat and add the tarragon.

5. Slice the roast and serve with the warm hollandaise.

PASTRAMI ROAST

 **MAKES 1 ROAST, ABOUT 8 SERVINGS**

WHILE WE HAVE A FEW ROAST recipes in the book, this is probably my favorite for grilling and my go-to to slice up for sandwiches. Rather than cooking it in salt water (as we do with our other roasts), here we create a flavored brine that uses sauerkraut juice and corning spices (the spices you use to make corned beef) to get that smoky pastrami flavor. You can pull the Pastrami Roast out in the morning to make bacon by thinly slicing it and baking it in the oven until it gets nice and crisp. Then come lunchtime, it's all about the Burnt Ends Biscuit Sandwich (page 78).

DRY MIXTURE

2⅓ cups vital wheat gluten

¼ cup garbanzo flour

VEGETABLES

¼ cup coconut oil

2 onions, minced

¼ cup sun-dried tomatoes, chopped, soaked in hot water for 5 minutes

¼ cup sauerkraut, minced

6 cloves garlic, minced

2 tablespoons vegan chicken base

2 teaspoons sea salt

2 teaspoons caraway seeds

2 bay leaves

LIQUID INGREDIENTS

½ cup tomato sauce

1¼ cups vegan vegetable stock, cold

¼ cup red wine

¼ cup tamari or soy sauce

1 tablespoon sesame oil

COOKING LIQUID

3 quarts water

1½ tablespoons sea salt

1 cup liquid from the sauerkraut jar

1 cup cider vinegar

1 tablespoon coriander seeds

4 bay leaves

1 tablespoon mustard seeds

2 teaspoons black peppercorns

2 teaspoons whole cloves

1 teaspoon allspice berries

RUB

2 teaspoons Chinese five-spice powder

1 tablespoon freshly ground black pepper

1 teaspoon dried ginger

2 teaspoons smoked paprika

EQUIPMENT

1 (24 x 18-inch) piece cheesecloth, folded in half to make a 12 x 18-inch piece

Safflower or canola oil spray

48 inches butcher's twine

1. Whisk the dry ingredients together in a large bowl.

2. In a skillet over medium heat, heat the coconut oil and add all the vegetable ingredients. Sauté for 20 minutes, stirring occasionally. Remove from the heat, discard the bay leaves, and cool in the fridge.

3. Combine the liquid ingredients in a large bowl and add the cooled vegetable mixture; mix together. Pour the liquid into the bowl of dry ingredients and stir together with a large spoon, then knead it lightly with your hands. The dough will be soft.

4. Combine the water and salt in a large stockpot, and bring to a boil.

5. Lay out the cheesecloth on a clean board and spray with oil. Form the dough into a roast shape and place it on one end of the cheesecloth. Roll up the roast in the cheesecloth, keeping it roast-shaped. Cut two pieces of twine, one about 10 inches long, the other 18 inches. Twist one end of the cheesecloth to make it tight against the roast, and using the 10-inch piece of string, tie this off with a double knot. Push in the roast on the untied end, and twist the cheesecloth until the roast is snug. Tie this off, using the 18-inch piece of string, with a double knot, tying off a loop at the end to use as a handle. Tie the roast with the remaining 20 inches of string at four equidistant intervals down the roast, using a slipknot (see How to Tie a Roast photos, page 15).

6. In a small pan over medium-low heat, slowly toast the cooking liquid spices; this should take 4 to 5 minutes. The spices will become fragrant. Add the spices to the cooking liquid. Bring to a boil.

7. Holding the tied end of the roast, gently lower it into the boiling water, adjusting the heat to keep the water at an aggressive simmer. Cover and simmer for 1½ hours, or until internally it reads 180°F on an instant-read thermometer, turning over halfway through the cooking process. Remove from the liquid and allow to cool at room temperature.

8. Combine the rub spices.

9. When the roast is cool enough to handle, remove the cheesecloth and rub the roast with spices.

10. Serve right away or finish cooling in the fridge. Wrap tightly in plastic wrap when fully cooled. The roast is ready to eat, and can be sliced thin for sandwiches, roasted with vegetables, or incorporated in the recipes in this book or your own favorites.

ISLAND-STYLE COCONUT DIPPERS

A SUPERVERSATILE FILLING for wraps and sandwiches and a great addition to salads or bento boxes, these dippers are like a vegan version of a coconut prawn. The great thing about them is you can cut them to the exact size you want: nugget-size for kid-friendly dinners, or strips or even steak-size for larger meals. If you're serving them straight up, sweet-and-sour sauce is a condiment of choice around here, as is our Avocado Ranch Dressing (page 198). And since they keep in the fridge for at least five days, they're the perfect candidate for stocking up for the busy week ahead.

2¼ cups unsweetened plain almond milk or water

2¼ cups all-purpose flour

2 tablespoons sea salt

1 tablespoon onion powder

1 teaspoon garlic powder

1 tablespoon curry powder

⅔ cup dried shredded coconut

1½ cups vegan panko bread crumbs

2 tablespoons sesame seeds

1 Lemongrass and Ginger Roast (page 18) or Lentil Sage Quarter Loaf, sliced into ½-inch pieces

3 cups safflower or another high-heat oil, such as canola, peanut, or vegetable, for frying

Sweet chili sauce

1. In a large bowl, whisk together the milk, 2 cups of the flour, and the salt, onion powder, garlic powder, and curry powder until fully combined.

2. In a separate bowl, mix together the coconut, bread crumbs, remaining ¼ cup of flour, and sesame seeds until fully combined.

3. Dip the roast or loaf pieces into the milk mixture to coat evenly. Transfer a slice to the bread crumb mixture and toss to coat. Transfer the breaded piece to a plate. Repeat until all the pieces are breaded. Place the plate in the fridge and chill for 30 minutes before frying.

4. Heat the oil to 350°F in a deep fryer or Dutch oven.

5. Fry each breaded slice for 3 to 4 minutes, or until golden brown. Transfer to a paper towel–lined plate to absorb excess oil. Serve hot with sweet chili sauce.

CHEF'S NOTE: *Slices of roast or loaf can be cut in half again to make bite-size pieces if you prefer.*

SCHWARTZWALDER SCHNITZEL

Our homage to the popular Bavarian dish, schnitzel at its simplest is essentially a cut of meat that's pounded thinly, then breaded and fried. Traditionally you'd use an egg dip to dredge the meat—first dipping it in flour, then egg, and then bread crumbs—but because we're cooking vegan here, I use a vegan egg (I like Follow Your Heart brand; see Sources, page 211). Schnitzel is often served with roasted cabbage, or it'd be great with my German Potato Salad (page 121) or Parsnip Root Whip (page 140), too. As with most regional favorites, there are many different varieties, but our schnitzel is a little easier as we get around the pounding step by using our Mushroom and Herb Roast (page 24) and thinly slicing it before dredging and frying.

¾ cup all-purpose flour

2 teaspoons sea salt

1 teaspoon celery salt

4 tablespoons Follow Your Heart vegan egg

1¼ cups unsweetened plain almond milk, cold

1½ cups vegan bread crumbs, processed in food processor until fine

2 teaspoons onion powder

1 tablespoon garlic powder

2 teaspoons paprika

2 teaspoons freshly ground black pepper

1 pound Mushroom and Herb Roast (page 24) or Field Roast Celebration Roast, sliced into ½-inch-thick steaks

¾ cup safflower oil

¾ cup Mushroom and Herb Stock (page 196) or vegan mushroom stock, warmed

½ cup vegan sour cream

1 lemon, sliced

1. In three medium-size bowls, create three different mixtures. The first: the flour, 2 teaspoons of the salt, and the celery salt. The second: the vegan egg and milk, whisked vigorously. The third: the bread crumbs, onion powder, garlic powder, paprika, and pepper.

2. Dredge each steak in the flour mixture, then the egg mixture, and then the bread crumb mixture, coating each steak evenly with each mixture (see Chef's Note).

3. In a skillet over medium-high heat, heat the safflower oil. When the oil is hot, begin frying the schnitzel three or four at a time, for about 3 minutes per side, or until golden brown. Transfer to a heatproof plate, and keep warm in an oven heated to 180°F.

4. Lower the skillet heat to medium-low and pour out any excess oil, but do not wipe out the pan. Add the mushroom stock, stir until hot, and then add the sour cream while continuing to whisk. Remove from the heat when fully combined. Serve the schnitzel with the sauce and lemon slices.

CHEF'S NOTE: *When you're dredging ingredients in the kitchen, set up your area neatly and try to get into the habit of one hand touching only dry ingredients and the other hand touching only wet ingredients. That way you'll finish the recipe with much cleaner hands, and a cleaner, more organized workspace, to boot!*

BOUND GROUNDS: GRIND, SAUSAGES, MEATLOAF, BURGERS, PÂTÉ

GRAIN MEAT GRIND

T HIS GROUND MEAT IS A workhorse for us here at Field Roast, and is the base for many of the recipes in this book. The reason I get so jazzed about our grind is that we use a double cooking process, which makes for a really tender, chewy texture that's just begging to be folded into your favorite recipes at home. Essentially, the mixture is cooked for the first time while you're making the meat grind, and for the second time in the recipe you ultimately use it in (meatloaf, roasts, sausages, etc.). Because it's so versatile, feel free to double the recipe and freeze it, ground, in resealable plastic bags for up to three months.

3¾ cups cold water

½ cup vegetable or vegan chicken base

3 tablespoons sea salt

4 cups vital wheat gluten

2 (24 x 18-inch) pieces cheesecloth, each folded in half to make a 12 x 18-inch piece

Safflower or canola oil spray

144 inches (8 feet) butcher's twine

1. In a large container, combine the cold water and base. In a mixing bowl, stir together the salt and the vital wheat gluten, then add the base mixture, mixing until combined. You may need to use your hands to bring everything together. This dough should look a little rough and may have a small amount of excess liquid in the bowl.

2. Divide the dough into two equal parts. Roll each half into a log about 8 inches long.

3. Lay out the cheesecloth on a clean counter or cutting board. Spray with oil and place each roll onto its own piece of cheesecloth. Wrap the cheesecloth around the roll. Cut four pieces of twine, two about 10 inches long, the other two 18 inches each. Twist one end of the cheesecloth to make it tight against the roll, and tie this off with a double knot, using a 10-inch piece of string. Push in the roll on the untied end, and twist the cheesecloth until the roll is snug. Tie this off, using an 18-inch piece of string with a double knot, tying off a loop at the end to use as a handle. Tie the other roll in the same manner. Cut the remaining piece of string in half (you will have two 20-inch pieces of string). Tie each roll with string at equidistant intervals down the roast, using a slipknot (see How to Tie a Roast photos, page 15).

4. In a large stockpot, bring 4 quarts of water to a boil. Holding the tied-off ends, gently slip the rolls into the water. Allow to come back to a boil, lower the heat to medium, and allow to simmer for about 1½ hours, or until internally it reads 195°F on an instant-read thermometer.

5. Remove each roll from the water and allow to cool enough to handle. Using scissors, cut away the twine and cheesecloth and discard.

6. Cut each loaf into 1-inch cubes. Run the cubes through a meat grinder or meat grinder attachment.

7. The rolls can be stored in a gallon-size resealable plastic bag in the freezer, or can be ground immediately to use in recipes.

CHEF'S NOTE: *When you first mix the ingredients together, do so with a spoon, but then feel free to dive in with your hands and get messy—it's simply easier to incorporate all the ingredients this way. The first time you make the meat grind, you'll likely feel like there's way too much water in the bowl, but don't worry: the gluten will absorb the liquid as it sits and you'll soon be left with a nice, uniform dough. If you do end up having excess moisture in the bowl, you'll just lift out the dough and leave it behind—nothing to worry about.*

FENNEL AND GARLIC SAUSAGE

I FIND LITTLE ELSE AS SATISFYING in the kitchen as making my own sausage, and this Mediterranean-inspired recipe is a great first foray. This sausage features two types of fennel: the actual bulb and fennel seeds, so it's really rich with that warm anise flavor but is balanced beautifully thanks to a generous smattering of Mediterranean herbs—and lots of garlic. I love this sausage sliced and tossed into pastas, but in truth, it needs little adornment: it's perfect grilled all on its own with seasonal salads and your favorite beer. Please note that our sausage recipes do require some special equipment and cooking instructions, which you can learn more about in Making Great Sausage at Home (page 12).

---

3 cups Grain Meat Grind (page 36)

VEGETABLE MIXTURE

1 yellow onion, ¼-inch diced

1 large or 2 small fennel bulbs, cored and
 ¼-inch diced

8 cloves garlic, minced

1 tablespoon olive oil

2 teaspoons salt

2 tablespoons vegan chicken base

DRY MIXTURE

1 tablespoon fennel seeds

2 teaspoons red pepper flakes

1 tablespoon dried oregano

1 tablespoon dried basil

2 teaspoons sea salt

2 teaspoons garlic powder

2 teaspoons sugar

2 teaspoons freshly ground black pepper

1 teaspoon dried marjoram

LIQUID MIXTURE

½ cup water

2 tablespoons olive oil

½ cup red wine

FINAL ADDITION

1¼ cups vital wheat gluten

EQUIPMENT

½ length sausage casing (about 5 inches
 still compressed; see note page 6) or
 24 inches aluminum foil or waxed paper

24 inches butcher's twine

Sausage stuffer or sausage stuffer
 attachment

Steamer basket

---

1. Place the grind in a large mixing bowl and set aside.

2. In a skillet over medium heat, sauté the vegetable mixture for 10 minutes, stirring occasionally, until the onion is translucent. Remove from the heat and cool in the fridge. When the vegetables are cool enough to handle, add them to the grind in the mixing bowl.

3. Combine the dry mixture ingredients in a small bowl, then combine with the grind mixture. Toss to coat thoroughly.

4. Whisk together the liquid mixture in a small bowl and combine with the grind mixture, stirring together with a large spoon. Add the vital wheat gluten and combine fully with your hands.

5. Extrude the sausage into the casing, tying it off with the butcher's twine. (Alternatively, see "Making Great Sausage at Home," page 12, if you do not have casing.) The sausages should not be stuffed too tightly, or else they will burst during the cooking process.

6. Steam the sausages in a steamer basket for 1 hour, then transfer to the fridge to cool. When the sausages are cool enough to handle, carefully remove the casing, and store the sausages in a resealable plastic bag in the fridge until ready to use.

NO MEAT GRINDER? NO PROBLEM

I realize that a meat grinder isn't exactly a mainstay in most home kitchens, so a good hack here is to use your food processor to grind the grain meat. To do so, slice up your meat into roughly 1-inch cubes and divide them into two groups. Because you want some differently sized bits in your grind for optimal texture, you're going to process one group into more of a fine grind (resembling, say, orzo pasta) and the other into more of a coarse grind (resembling a small bean). Once the meat is processed, you'll go ahead and mix both grinds together in a big bowl, and you're ready to roll.

SMOKED POTATO AND ARTICHOKE SAUSAGE

MILDER THAN OUR OTHER SAUSAGES with a natural sweetness and a little smokiness, these make great breakfast sausages and tend to be a hit at the kid's table, too. We don't use fresh herbs in any of our other sausage recipes, but I love the dill here for its brightness and the way it complements the flavors of the tender potatoes and artichoke. You can grill these superversatile sausages, freeze them for later, or do as I do and use them up in your favorite sandwiches, pastas, or scrambles. It's hard to go wrong.

3 cups Grain Meat Grind (page 36)

VEGETABLE MIXTURE

1 medium-size yellow onion, ¼-inch diced

1 (14-ounce) can artichoke hearts,
    drained, rinsed, and chopped into
    ¼-inch pieces

8 cloves garlic, minced

1 tablespoon olive oil

2 teaspoons salt

2 tablespoons vegan chicken base

DRY MIXTURE

¼ cup light brown sugar

2 teaspoons red pepper flakes

1 tablespoon dried rubbed sage

1 tablespoon dried basil

2 teaspoons sea salt

2 teaspoons garlic powder

2 teaspoons granulated sugar

2 teaspoons freshly ground black pepper

2 teaspoons dried thyme

1 teaspoon smoked paprika

LIQUID MIXTURE

½ cup water

2 tablespoons olive oil

½ cup white wine

1 yellow potato, ⅛-inch diced

8 sprigs dill, large stems removed and
    fronds minced

1 teaspoon liquid smoke

FINAL ADDITION

1¼ cups vital wheat gluten

EQUIPMENT

½ length sausage casing (about 5 inches
    still compressed; see note page 6) or
    24 inches aluminum foil or waxed paper

24 inches butcher's twine

Sausage stuffer or sausage stuffer
    attachment

1. Place the grind in a large mixing bowl and set aside.

2. In a skillet over medium heat, sauté the vegetable mixture for 10 minutes, stirring occasionally, until the onion is translucent. Remove from the heat and cool in the fridge. When the vegetables are cool enough to handle, add them to the grind in the mixing bowl.

3. Combine the dry mixture ingredients in a small bowl, then combine with the grind mixture. Toss to coat thoroughly.

4. Whisk together the liquid mixture in a small bowl and combine with the grind mixture, stirring together with a large spoon. Add the vital wheat gluten and combine fully with your hand.

5. Extrude the sausage into the casing, tying it off with the butcher's twine. (Alternatively, see "Making Great Sausage at Home," page 12, if you do not have casing.) The sausages should not be stuffed too tightly, or else they will burst during the cooking process.

6. Steam the sausages for 1 hour, then transfer to the fridge to cool.

7. When the sausages are cool enough to handle carefully remove the casing, and store the sausages in a resealable plastic bag in the fridge until ready to use.

CHEF'S NOTE: *A few things will really help make your life easy when filling the casing with this sausage mixture. First, we don't precook the potato for this sausage because it'd just fall apart when you go to put it in the casing. Second, you want to make sure to dice your potato to the point where it'll still go through the sausage horn or, similarly, it'll get stuck.*

OAXACAN CHILI-SPICED SAUSAGE

T HE WONDERFUL THING ABOUT making sausage at home is that you can control the level of spice and seasoning, and here, in our homage to a spicy chorizo, that's truer than ever. A robust, slightly tangy sausage, you've got the possibility for serious heat here thanks to the cayenne and chili oil, but you could also scale back and test the waters before fully diving in. The beauty is in the tweaking, and in making it a little bit different each time—until you get it just right. Because the recipe calls for a good bit of chili oil, when the sausage is ground down, a lot of those oils are released and help to flavor whatever you're adding it to. Might I suggest casseroles, soups, and stews, or morning scrambles and breakfast burritos? Please note that our sausage recipes do require some special equipment and cooking instructions, which you can learn more about in Making Great Sausage at Home (page 12).

3 cups Grain Meat Grind (page 36)

VEGETABLE MIXTURE

1 tablespoon olive oil

1 yellow onion, ¼-inch diced

1 chipotle pepper in adobo

12 cloves garlic, minced

2 tablespoons vegetable base

DRY MIXTURE

1 tablespoon dark brown sugar

2 teaspoons dried oregano

2 tablespoons smoked paprika

2 teaspoons sea salt

2 teaspoons garlic powder

1 teaspoon freshly ground black pepper

2 teaspoons chili powder

2 teaspoons ground cumin

½ teaspoons cayenne pepper

2 teaspoons dried thyme

LIQUID MIXTURE

¾ cup water

2 tablespoons olive oil

¼ cup cider vinegar

1 teaspoon liquid smoke

FINAL ADDITION

1¼ cups vital wheat gluten

EQUIPMENT

½ length sausage casing (about 5 inches still compressed; see note page 6) or 24 inches aluminum foil or waxed paper

24 inches butcher's twine

Sausage stuffer or sausage stuffer attachment

1. Place the grind in a large mixing bowl and set aside.

2. In a skillet over medium heat, heat the oil and add the rest of the vegetable mixture. Sauté for 10 minutes, stirring occasionally, until the onion is translucent. Remove from the heat and cool in the fridge. When the vegetables are cool enough to handle, add them to the grind in the mixing bowl.

3. Combine the dry mixture ingredients in a small bowl, then combine with the grind mixture. Toss to coat thoroughly.

4. Whisk together the liquid mixture in a small bowl and combine with the grind mixture, stirring together with a large spoon. Add the vital wheat gluten and combine fully with your hands.

5. Extrude the sausage into the casing, tying it off with the butcher's twine. (Alternatively, see "Making Great Sausage at Home," page 12, if you do not have casing.) The sausages should not be stuffed too tightly, or else they will burst during the cooking process.

6. Steam the sausages for 1 hour, then transfer to the fridge to cool.

7. When the sausages are cool enough to handle, carefully remove the casing, and store the sausages in a resealable plastic bag in the fridge until ready to use.

CHEF'S NOTE: *Chili oil is renowned for staining cutting boards, so don't use your very favorite board to prep this sausage.*

LITTLE SAIGON MEATLOAF

MOST OF THE VIETNAMESE DELIS here in Seattle do a pretty standard Asian-style meatloaf, and while they are delicious, I've long wanted to do a vegan version. Although you're likely familiar with the flavors of a real down-home American meatloaf, giving it a Vietnamese twist by reaching for lemongrass stalks, galangal (see Chef's Note), and small Asian eggplant makes this recipe truly stand out. At home we make this meatloaf and slice it to use on sandwiches throughout the week or break out the BBQ sauce and serve it warm with roasted potatoes and veggies. Admittedly, it's very different from the meatloaf I grew up with, but it's where I turn for comfort food today.

VEGETABLES

2 teaspoons sesame oil

2 tablespoons olive oil

¾ cup Asian eggplant, peeled and ¼-inch diced

1 (3-inch) section lemongrass stalk

½ cup minced onion

2 tablespoons minced galangal

1 tablespoon tamari

1 tablespoon vegan beef base

ADDITIONAL GRIND INGREDIENTS

2 cups Grain Meat Grind (page 36), ground

2½ tablespoons tomato paste

2 teaspoons onion powder

1 tablespoon garlic, minced

1 tablespoon curry powder

1 teaspoon star anise

½ teaspoon black pepper

1 teaspoon cayenne pepper

½ teaspoon red pepper flakes

1 tablespoon vegan Worcestershire sauce

BINDER

¼ cup coconut oil, melted

3 tablespoons olive oil

1¾ cups vital wheat gluten

ACTIVATOR

¼ cup water

EQUIPMENT

2 (6-inch) loaf pans

Steamer basket

1. In a skillet over medium heat, heat the sesame and olive oil and add all the vegetable ingredients, including the base. Sauté, stirring occasionally, for 4 minutes. Remove from the heat and transfer the mixture from the skillet to a large mixing bowl.

2. Add the grind and its additional ingredients to the vegetables in the mixing bowl, and stir to combine.

3. In a bowl, combine the binder ingredients and mix well with a spoon. The mixture should become thick like batter.

4. Scoop the binder mixture over the grind mixture. Combine the mixtures thoroughly by hand. Do not skip this step, or add water beforehand, or the recipe will not work.

5. When the mixtures are fully combined, sprinkle the activator water over the top and mix again, using your hands.

6. Form the mixture into two equal-size loaves and transfer to the loaf pans.

7. Steam the loaves in a steamer basket over 4 inches of water for 2 hours, monitoring the amount of water in the pot below and adding more, if needed. Remove from the steamer, and allow to fully cool. When the loaves are cool, they may be glazed and roasted, sliced for sandwiches, or used for another recipe.

CHEF'S NOTE: *Galangal is essentially Thai ginger and is a bit spicier and more pungent than traditional fresh ginger. It's available at most Asian food markets and natural foods stores. If you have trouble finding it, feel free to use regular fresh ginger instead. For tips on working with lemongrass, see page 9.*

BOUND BY GLUTEN

Generally when we make grain meats, we incorporate all the ingredients with the fat, adding the gluten last to make sure they bind together into a cohesive mixture. Why? Because when the water hits the gluten, the gluten becomes activated and everything begins to come together. The proteins contained in the vital wheat gluten react with the water and begin to align, forming tight elastic bonds that keep our meats from falling apart. Unlike our general grain meat method (see note on page 36) with our meatloaf, burger, and pâté recipes we want to get the gluten bonded with the fat first, before we add the water; we add the fat straight to the gluten and mix to make it pourable. Then, when we add the water and activate the gluten, the fat is distributed evenly throughout. This results in juicy, fattier meats, whose fat will remain attached to the protein during cooking, rather than running out. This method is responsible for those great burger characteristics: superjuicy, grillable, meaty texture that tastes really, really great.

PÂTÉ DE CAMPAGNE

O N T H E R A R E O C C A S I O N W H E N I feel the need for a very special appetizer, I turn to this pâté. It's pretty fatty, as pâté is known to be, so I like to serve it along with a vegan cheese and something light, such as our Céleri Rémoulade (page 126). Have some fun with the mushrooms here, swapping out different varieties based on what you find at the store or what you're into. Feel free to use brandy instead of cognac, and if you're feeling especially fancy, use a little truffle oil instead of olive oil. The pâté keeps in the fridge for four to five days, although it never lasts that long in our house.

VEGETABLE MIXTURE

2 tablespoons olive oil

1 medium-size yellow onion, minced

½ pound shiitake mushrooms, stems removed, caps ¼-inch diced

2 teaspoons sea salt

1 cup Grain Meat Grind (page 36)

ADDITIONAL FLAVORING INGREDIENTS

1 tablespoon tomato paste

Leaves from 3 sprigs tarragon, minced

2 medium-size caps dried morel mushrooms, soaked in hot water for 5 minutes, drained, and minced

1 tablespoon vegan chicken base

1 teaspoon onion powder

2 cloves garlic, minced

Leaves from 3 sprigs thyme

½ teaspoon dried marjoram

½ teaspoon dried rubbed sage

Pinch of ground cloves

Pinch of ground nutmeg

Pinch of ground coriander

Pinch of ground white pepper

Pinch of ground cinnamon

½ teaspoon freshly ground black pepper

BINDER

2 tablespoons coconut oil, melted

1 tablespoon olive oil

1 teaspoon sesame oil

1 cup vital wheat gluten

ACTIVATOR

1 ounce cognac

1 tablespoon tamari

EQUIPMENT

1 (6-inch) loaf pan

Waxed paper

Steamer basket

1. In a skillet over medium heat, heat the olive oil, then add all the remaining vegetable mixture ingredients, except the grind. Cook for 15 to 20 minutes, or until the liquid is gone and the onion has fully browned. Transfer to a large mixing bowl and add the grind.

2. Add the additional flavoring ingredients to the grind mixture and stir to fully combine everything.

3. In a separate bowl, combine the binder ingredients, and whisk until a loose paste forms. Spoon this paste over the top of the grind mixture. Use your hands to mix together until everything is fully combined.

4. Combine the cognac and tamari in a small bowl to create the gluten activator.

5. Sprinkle the activator over the top of the grind mixture and combine again. Press the mixture down into the loaf pan and cover with a piece of waxed paper.

6. Transfer the pan to a steamer basket placed over water that is at a low boil. Steam for 1 hour 45 minutes. Remove from the heat, place the loaf pan in the fridge, and chill overnight.

SERVING SUGGESTIONS: *Serve with crackers and Céleri Rémoulade (page 126).*

PEPPER-STUFFED BURGERS

WITH ALL OF OUR BURGERS, we aim to get that nice grilled exterior with a juicy burst of flavor on the inside, and a great way to do that is with a stuffed burger. As for timing and executing, do take a little time reading through this recipe, as it has a few steps: you're going to make the burger meat first, then the stuffing, and then put the whole thing together. And then when you try your first bite, you'll make plans to start the process all over again.

STUFFING

3 pepperoncini, minced

1 medium-size jalapeño pepper, minced

1 teaspoon fennel seeds

1 red bell pepper, seeded and minced

1 teaspoon dried oregano

1 teaspoon olive oil

2 cloves garlic, minced

1 teaspoon sea salt

¼ cup vegan bread crumbs

VEGETABLE MIXTURE

2 tablespoons olive oil

¾ cup minced cremini mushrooms

½ cup minced onion

½ cup minced fennel bulb

2 teaspoons sea salt

1 tablespoon vegan beef base

ADDITIONAL GRIND INGREDIENTS

2 cups Grain Meat Grind (page 36), ground

2½ tablespoons tomato paste

2 teaspoons onion powder

1 tablespoon minced garlic

1 teaspoon dried oregano

1 teaspoon dried thyme

½ teaspoon freshly ground black pepper

½ teaspoon liquid smoke

½ teaspoon red pepper flakes

1 tablespoon vegan Worcestershire sauce

BINDER

¼ cup coconut oil, melted

3 tablespoons olive oil

1¾ cups vital wheat gluten

ACTIVATOR

¼ cup water

EQUIPMENT

Waxed paper or plastic wrap

8 (3½-inch-diameter) English muffin rings or similar

Steamer basket

1. In a medium-size bowl, combine the stuffing ingredients and set aside.

2. In a skillet over medium heat, heat the olive oil and add the remaining vegetable ingredients, including the base. Sauté, stirring occasionally, for 4 minutes. Remove from the heat and transfer the mixture from the skillet to a large mixing bowl.

3. Add the additional grind ingredients to the vegetables in the mixing bowl and stir to combine.

4. In a bowl, combine the binder ingredients, mixing well with a spoon. The mixture should become thick like batter.

5. Scoop the binder mixture over the grind mixture. Combine the mixtures thoroughly by hand. Do not skip this step, or add water beforehand, or the recipe will not work.

6. When the mixtures are fully combined, sprinkle the activator water over the top and mix again using your hands.

7. Form the mixture into a roll and, using a sharp knife, slice into eight equal rounds. Place the rounds on some waxed paper or plastic wrap, and press each round down into a burger shape.

8. Lay out four rounds and spoon a 1-inch ping-pong ball sized mound of stuffing onto the middle of each round. Top each round with another round, and pinch the sides together all the way around each burger.

9. Place each burger in a 3½-inch-diameter, 1-inch-high ring, and press down. I use English muffin rings, but any rings about the same size will do. Move each ring to a steamer basket over boiling water and steam for 1 hour.

10. Remove the burgers from the steamer and allow to cool. Remove the burgers from the rings. The burgers can be wrapped in plastic wrap and kept in the fridge for up to 5 days.

CHEF'S NOTE: *To give these burgers form and shape while they cook, I use a 3½-inch-diameter English muffin ring that you can find at most kitchen supply stores. You can certainly go bigger or smaller, but you are going to want something round to form and cook each burger in.*

BREAKFAST

CHICKEN-FRIED SAUSAGE AND WAFFLES

L OS ANGELES REALLY IS the home of chicken and waffles, so when I was asked to make a vegan food option for an LA-based conference, I thought why not do a killer vegan version that everyone would love? The waffle recipe itself is made with ground flax instead of eggs and a little whole wheat flour—they're buttery and crisp and delicious. And the meat portion is inspired by Ezell's, a much-beloved fried chicken spot in Seattle. I worked to deconstruct Ezell's recipe and found that the secret to getting that supercrispy crunch is crushed cornflakes. For my plant-based version I use our sausage for the dark meat and maitake mushrooms (otherwise known as hen of the woods) for the light meat. The takeaway: if you're wondering what to make to turn someone on to vegan food, this recipe has a 100 percent success rate. Just saying.

SAUSAGE AND MUSHROOM FRY

1½ cups unsweetened plain almond milk, cold

3 tablespoons Follow Your Heart vegan egg

1¾ cups all-purpose flour

2 teaspoons celery salt

2 teaspoons garlic powder

2 teaspoons smoked paprika

2 teaspoons curry powder

2 teaspoons freshly ground black pepper

1 tablespoon dried rubbed sage

2 teaspoons onion powder

1 tablespoon plus one teaspoon sea salt

2 cups cornflakes, pulsed in a food processor or crushed using the bottom of a glass

2 links Smoked Potato and Artichoke Sausage (page 40) or Field Roast Smoked Apple Sage Sausage, sliced on the bias into ⅔-inch-thick pieces

1 (3½-ounce) bunch maitake mushrooms, divided into 2-inch pieces

WAFFLES, DRY INGREDIENTS

1¼ cups all-purpose flour

¼ cup whole wheat flour

2 tablespoons ground flaxseeds

1 teaspoon baking powder

1 teaspoon sea salt

WAFFLES, WET INGREDIENTS

4 teaspoons sugar

¼ cup pure maple syrup

¼ cup vegan butter, melted

2 cups unsweetened plain almond milk

2 tablespoons safflower oil

1 tablespoon pure vanilla extract

4 cups safflower or another high-heat oil, such as canola, peanut, or vegetable, for frying

Safflower or canola oil spray

GARNISH

Pure maple syrup

Vegan butter

1. In a blender, blend together the milk and vegan egg until fully combined, about 2 minutes. Pour the mixture into a medium-size bowl.

2. In a large bowl, whisk together 1 cup of the flour and the celery salt, garlic powder, paprika, curry powder, pepper, sage, onion powder, and 1 tablespoon of the salt. Add the cornflakes and stir to combine.

3. In a separate bowl, whisk together the remaining ¾ cup flour and remaining teaspoon of salt and set aside.

4. Take a piece of sausage and lightly press down on the flat side so it loses about half its height and has less of a rigid shape. Repeat the process with the rest of the sausage pieces.

5. To bread the sausage and the mushrooms, dip first into the bowl of salted flour to fully coat. Shake off any excess flour and transfer the piece to the milk mixture, being careful not to get your hand wet. Using your opposite hand, retrieve the piece from the milk bowl and transfer it to the cornflake mixture, being careful not to dip that hand into the dry mixture. Using your dry hand, coat the piece with cornflake mixture on both sides, gently pressing down to ensure the coating has adhered to the piece. Transfer the finished pieces to a tray and set aside.

6. In a large bowl, whisk together the waffle dry ingredients. In a separate bowl, whisk together the waffle wet ingredients. Pour the wet mixture into the dry mixture and whisk gently, stopping just before everything is fully combined. Set aside.

7. Heat a waffle iron. In a deep fryer or Dutch oven, heat the frying oil to 375°F.

8. Spray the waffle iron with oil, pour in about ⅓ cup of batter, and close. Following the directions of the waffle iron manufacturer, cook until golden brown. Repeat until all the batter is cooked.

9. While the waffles are cooking, begin deep-frying the sausage and mushroom pieces, a few at a time, until golden brown. Transfer to a paper towel–lined plate.

10. Plate the fried sausage and mushroom pieces on top of the waffles and serve with maple syrup and vegan butter.

BISCUITS AND GRAVY WITH SPICY SAUSAGE AND CORN

 **MAKES 4 SERVINGS**

When I was little, my grandpa used to take me out to the Lions Club fund-raiser breakfasts where the menu options were delightfully predictable: pancakes or biscuits and gravy. I suppose I was similarly predictable as I always chose the latter, and while I realize you weren't there, I'm sure you can imagine that classic country gravy and those baking powder biscuits. Today these are really nostalgic for me, but that sausage gravy can get boring, so I put a Tex-Mex spin on it, subbing in our Oaxacan Chili-Spiced Sausage (page 42), and tossing in a little corn and smoked paprika. I'm not sure the Lions Club members would agree, but I assure you that dressing these up with a little hot sauce, salsa, and fresh avocado is always a good idea.

1 tablespoon safflower oil

1 medium-size shallot

2 cloves garlic, minced

7 ounces Oaxacan Chili-Spiced Sausage (page 42) or 2 links Field Roast Mexican Chipotle Sausage, crumbled

¼ cup vegan butter

3 tablespoons all-purpose flour

2½ cups unsweetened plain almond milk, warmed

2 teaspoons sea salt

1 tablespoon vegan Worcestershire sauce

2 teaspoons smoked paprika

Leaves from 3 sprigs thyme

½ cup corn kernels, frozen or fresh, removed from the cob

4 Genesee Biscuits (page 201)

4 green onions, thinly sliced

1. In a skillet over medium heat, heat the safflower oil. Add the shallot, garlic, and sausage. Sauté, stirring occasionally, for 10 minutes, until the shallot is translucent. Remove the mixture from the pan and set aside. Return the pan to the heat and add the butter and flour. Using a wooden spoon, move the mixture around, as it cooks, for 5 minutes, then add the milk. Begin whisking the mixture; as it starts to thicken, add the sausage mixture back to the pan. Add the salt, Worcestershire, paprika, thyme, and corn. Stir, and lower the heat to low.

2. Warm the biscuits and split in half. Top each with a generous portion of gravy and garnish with green onions.

TOMATO LOX AND CREAM
CHEESE BAGELS, PAGE 58

TOMATO LOX AND CREAM CHEESE BAGELS

 **MAKES 4 SERVINGS**

GROWING UP AS A PACIFIC NORTHWEST KID, I ate a lot of seafood. On top of that, my grandpa and both of my parents have in some way been involved in the seafood industry for my entire life. Salmon is such a symbol for the Northwest, most Seattle schools teach their students how local tribes would dry or smoke salmon on special racks to preserve the food through the tough winters. I wanted to include an homage to the local and my personal culinary heritage in this book; this recipe will show you how to infuse some less-than-ripe vegetables with delicious smoky flavor, so you can enjoy a local Northwest favorite, bagels with lox. Some plant-based chefs have made a vegan lox using carrots, but I was drawn to slightly underripe tomatoes. We've all seen them in the grocery store, tomatoes that are, sadly, more pink than red, and I figured their color would be perfect—and it is. As always, feel free to customize here and use your favorite seasonal vegetables, sprouts, a smattering of fresh herbs, or your favorite cream cheese.

---

4 whole, firm, medium-size on-the-vine tomatoes

¼ cup tamari or soy sauce

½ teaspoon liquid smoke

1 teaspoon sugar

1 teaspoon sesame oil

1 teaspoon safflower oil

½ small beet, boiled for 15 minutes, peeled, and sliced into ⅛-inch-thick slices

4 vegan bagels, sliced in half

5 ounces vegan cream cheese

¼ cup capers

½ medium-size red onion, sliced into ⅛-inch slices

6 sprigs dill

---

1. In a medium-size saucepan, bring 2 quarts of water to a boil. In a large mixing bowl, combine 2 quarts of cold water with a quart of ice. Drop the tomatoes into the boiling water, and let them cook, until you see the skin split. Remove the tomatoes and transfer to the cold water.

2. In another bowl, combine the tamari, liquid smoke, sugar, sesame oil, and safflower oil and stir well. Add the beet slices and toss to coat. Set aside.

3. Peel the skins off the tomatoes and discard. Quarter each tomato, and using a sharp knife, slice away the inner membrane and remove the seeds, leaving the meaty outer wall of the tomato flesh. Transfer these to the tamari mixture and toss to coat. Allow to soak for 1 hour before serving.

4. Toast each bagel half, and serve with cream cheese, capers, onion, marinated tomato pieces, and dill for garnish.

MIGAS

M IGAS IS A BREAKFAST DISH with utilitarian roots. Families that had too many tortillas left over from the previous day's meals would chop them up and cook them with eggs and chiles. This vegan version relies on tofu instead of eggs and plenty of salsa, sour cream, guacamole . . . and extra chips. Always extra chips.

2 Roma tomatoes, ¼-inch diced

2 cloves garlic, minced

3 tablespoons freshly squeezed lime juice

3 teaspoons sea salt

4 sprigs cilantro, large stems removed, minced

1 jalapeño pepper, minced

1 pound medium-soft tofu, patted dry and ¾-inch diced

¼ cup vegan mayo

2 teaspoons Follow Your Heart vegan egg (or substitute 1 teaspoon nutritional yeast plus 1 teaspoon turmeric)

2 tablespoons safflower oil

6 (6-inch) white corn tortillas, sliced into ½-inch strips

2 links Oaxacan Chili-Spiced Sausage (page 42) or Field Roast Mexican Chipotle Sausage, crumbled

1 medium-size yellow onion, ¼-inch diced

1 zucchini, ¼-inch diced

1 green bell pepper, ¼-inch diced

2 teaspoons chili powder

1 teaspoon ground cumin

1 avocado, peeled, pitted, and sliced

1. In a bowl, combine the tomatoes, half of the garlic, the lime juice, 1 teaspoon of the salt, the cilantro, and half of the jalapeño. Stir to mix, and set aside.

2. In a large mixing bowl, place the tofu, mayo, vegan egg (or nutritional yeast and turmeric, if using those instead), and 1 teaspoon of the salt. Using a large spoon or your hands, work the ingredients together, crumbling the tofu, and fully combining the ingredients. Set aside.

3. In a skillet over medium heat, heat the oil and add the tortilla strips. Using tongs, gently stir the tortillas every minute or so, until they begin to brown, 4 to 5 minutes. Transfer the strips to a paper towel–lined plate.

4. Return the skillet to the heat and add the sausage, onion, zucchini, bell pepper, remaining jalapeño, remaining garlic, chili powder, cumin, and remaining 1 teaspoon of salt. Stir this mixture to combine, and cook over medium heat, stirring occasionally, for 5 to 7 minutes, or until the onion is translucent. Add the tortilla strips and tofu mixture to the skillet and stir gently to combine.

5. Serve garnished with the tomato salsa and avocado.

SERVING SUGGESTION: *Serve with a side of beans or breakfast potatoes.*

FLORENTINE BENEDICT

I<small>N CASE YOU WERE CONCERNED</small>, I'm here to assure you that Seattle's brunch culture is alive and well. And while yogurt parfaits and avocado toast get a lot of play on restaurant menus, I think the classic eggs Benedict is where it's at. When I lived in the Capitol Hill neighborhood, I used to go to this great brunch spot that made a Florentine Benedict with spinach and tomatoes and it soon became the only thing I'd order. So, I set out to make a plant-based version of the recipe, using our Vegan Hollandaise (page 193) and ample fresh vegetables. I like to grill the tomatoes quickly to draw out some of their natural sweetness and quickly sauté the spinach to soften it up. And always a fan of saving time whenever possible, I generally make the sauce the night before, so that in the morning I'm just pulling together all the components, spending more time with friends and less time over the stove.

---

1 tablespoon safflower oil, plus 1 teaspoon for grilling tomatoes and sausage

2 cloves garlic

3 ounces baby spinach (about 4 cups)

3 tablespoons sherry

2 teaspoons sea salt

14 ounces Smoked Potato and Artichoke Sausage (page 40) or 4 links Field Roast Smoked Apple Sage Sausage,

sliced down the middle lengthwise, divided in half, and brushed with oil

2 whole, on-the-vine tomatoes, thickly sliced and brushed with oil

1 teaspoon freshly ground black pepper

4 vegan English muffins, sliced in half

1 tablespoon vegan butter, melted

2 cups Vegan Hollandaise (page 193)

---

1. In a skillet over medium heat, heat the safflower oil and add the garlic. Cook, stirring, for about 2 minutes, until the garlic becomes fragrant. Add the spinach, sherry, and 1 teaspoon of the salt, stir to combine, and cover. Allow to cook for 2 to 3 minutes; the spinach will be soft. Remove from the heat.

2. On a grill or in a skillet over high heat, grill the sausages, flat side down, for 5 minutes, or until hot throughout. Sprinkle the remaining teaspoon of salt and the pepper on the tomatoes and grill for 5 minutes.

3. Toast the English muffins and brush with melted butter.

4. Layer each English muffin half with a good spoonful of the spinach, then the tomato, and top with the sausage. Ladle ¼ cup of hot hollandaise sauce over the top of each half.

STRATA PROVENÇAL

IF YOU'RE NEW TO STRATA, I've got three words for you: breakfast bread pudding. A great way to use up your day-old bread, strata is a layered bread casserole that easily feeds a crowd and is a dish I really crave when comfort food is in order. There are many different recipes for strata, but this one is my favorite. I use our Fresh Herb Focaccia (page 202), fresh tarragon, a good Dijon mustard and our creamy Vegan Béchamel (page 192). But the stars here are the niçoise olives—they're small, salty, and pungent and add some nice balance and acidity to the creaminess of the dish.

¼ cup olive oil

1 medium-size to large fennel bulb, cored and sliced ⅛ inch thick

1 medium-size yellow onion, sliced into thin half-moons

3 ounces fresh spinach

¼ cup white wine

2 links Fennel and Garlic Sausage (page 38) or Field Roast Italian Sausage, thinly sliced or crumbled

1 tablespoon plus 1 teaspoon sea salt

2½ cups Vegan Béchamel (page 192), cold

1½ cups unsweetened plain almond milk, cold

¼ cup Follow Your Heart vegan egg

2 tablespoons Dijon mustard

Leaves from 4 sprigs tarragon

2 teaspoons freshly ground black pepper

½ cup niçoise olives, pitted

1 loaf Fresh Herb Focaccia (page 202) or other vegan focaccia bread (a day or two old, so it's crusty), cut into ¾-inch cubes

Safflower or canola oil spray

1. Preheat the oven to 375°F. In a large skillet over medium heat, heat the olive oil and add the fennel and onion. Sauté for 10 to 15 minutes, stirring occasionally. The onion will begin to become translucent. Add the spinach, wine, sausage, and 1 tablespoon of the salt, and increase the heat to medium-high. Continue to cook, stirring the mixture, so that the spinach wilts and most of the liquid is absorbed, another 5 to 6 minutes. Remove from the heat and set aside.

2. In a blender, combine the béchamel, milk, vegan egg, Dijon, remaining teaspoon of salt, tarragon, and pepper. Blend until fully combined, about 2 minutes.

3. In a large bowl, combine the béchamel mixture and the vegetable mixture. Add the olives and bread cubes and gently toss to coat. Spray a large baking dish (or two medium-size baking dishes) with oil, and add the strata mixture. Press the mixture down flat in the bowl; if it seems too dry, sprinkle a small amount of milk over the top. Allow this to sit for 20 minutes before baking, to allow the liquid to soak into the bread. Bake for 25 to 30 minutes. The bread should be golden brown and crusty on top and all the liquid should be absorbed. Allow to cool for 5 to 7 minutes before serving.

CHEF'S NOTE: *Allow yourself enough time here to let the liquid soak into the bread layers before baking—you want to give it a chance to absorb so all the flavors really develop and the dish bakes uniformly.*

GREEN MACHINE BREAKFAST BURRITO

 **MAKES 5 SERVINGS**

N‌O MATTER HOW MANY TIMES I hear how important breakfast is and how hard I try to jump on the bandwagon, my weekday mornings can sometimes consist solely of a hot cup of coffee for sustenance. I'm often in a hurry to hop on my bike and start the morning commute, and most cereals and morning pastries end up feeling heavy, so I started making these protein-packed breakfast burritos as a way to get in some much needed energy before my morning ride. Relying on collard leaves instead of tortillas, this recipe feels much lighter than your typical breakfast burrito and you can make a batch ahead of time, and wrap and refrigerate them for grab-and-go meals each morning. This recipe is infinitely adaptable, so I hope you'll make them your own: if you're not a fan of tofu, substitute chopped seasonal vegetables instead. Have leftover grains in the fridge? Feel free to toss in a handful or two. Love sriracha? Vegan cheese? You get the idea. Go to town.

---

5 large collard leaves

½ pound Yukon Gold potatoes, cut into ¼-inch pieces

2 tablespoons olive oil

½ pound firm tofu, crumbled

2 tablespoons vegan mayo

2 teaspoons mustard powder

¼ cup nutritional yeast

1 teaspoon ground turmeric

1 teaspoon sea salt

½ pound Oaxacan Chili-Spiced Sausage (page 42) or Field Roast Mexican Chipotle Sausage, crumbled

1 jalapeño pepper, minced (optional)

2 green onions, green tops sliced very thinly on the bias so they curl

1 cup baby spinach

1 Roma tomato, sliced

⅓ bunch cilantro, chopped

---

1. Preheat the oven to 400°F. Cut out and discard the collard stems from about a third of the way up each leaf and set the leaves aside.

2. Toss the potato in half of the oil and roast in the oven on a baking sheet for 15 minutes. Combine the tofu, mayo, mustard, nutritional yeast, turmeric, and the salt in a bowl and set aside.

3. In a skillet over medium heat, sauté the sausage, potato, jalapeño, green onion, and spinach, stirring occasionally, until spinach has cooked down, 7 to 10 minutes. Remove from the heat and set aside.

4. Lay out each collard leaf on a work surface and fill with one scoop of the tofu mixture and one scoop of the sausage mixture, then garnish with tomato and cilantro.

5. Roll up each leaf, stem side first, as you would a tortilla.

6. For added stability, wrap each burrito in plastic wrap and slice down the middle, peeling away the plastic as you eat.

ROASTED CHAYOTE BREAKFAST SKILLET

WE ALL LOVE BREAKFAST FOR DINNER on occasion, and when the craving strikes, this is the dish I turn to. Chayote is much like a summer squash or zucchini, but the flesh is a little tougher. It's used in a lot of Mexican cooking, and if you ask me, it's seriously underappreciated: I'm a fan. If you're craving more protein in this morning skillet, feel free to fold in the tofu scramble from the Migas recipe (page 59), or just add a few extra sausage links.

5 teaspoons sea salt

1 pound yam, peeled and ½-inch diced

1 pound Yukon Gold potatoes, ½-inch diced

1 chayote squash, seeded, cut into ½-inch chunks

½ cup safflower oil

7 to 8 medium-size tomatillos, papery outer skin removed

1 jalapeño pepper, sliced (optional)

1 tablespoon minced fresh ginger

Leaves from 4 sprigs cilantro, roughly chopped

¼ cup lime juice, freshly squeezed

2 cloves garlic

1 teaspoon sugar

1 red onion, ½-inch diced

1 red bell pepper, ½-inch diced

2 links Oaxacan Chili-Spiced Sausage (page 42) or Field Roast Mexican Chipotle Sausages, sliced

⅔ cup corn kernels, frozen or fresh, removed from the cob

1. Preheat the oven to 450°F. In a pot over high heat, bring 8 cups of water and 1 tablespoon of the salt to a boil. Add the yam and potato and boil for 5 minutes. Drain and set aside.

2. In a large bowl, toss the chayote with 2 teaspoons of the oil and 1 teaspoon of the salt. Transfer the squash to a baking dish and roast in the oven for 25 minutes. The squash will be tender but not soft all the way through.

3. In a large bowl, toss the tomatillos, 2 teaspoons of the oil, and remaining teaspoon of salt. Transfer the tomatillos to a baking dish and roast for 15 minutes. Remove from the oven and allow to cool slightly before transferring to a blender or food processor. Add the jalapeño, ginger, cilantro, lime juice, garlic, and sugar and process until all chunks are gone. Set aside.

4. In a large, ovenproof skillet over medium heat, heat the remaining oil, onion, red pepper, sausage, yam, and potato. Stir occasionally. After 4 minutes, add the squash and corn, stir, and transfer the pan to the oven to roast for 5 to 7 minutes.

5. Serve on a plate, or directly out of the skillet, with the tomatillo salsa on the side.

CHEF'S NOTE: *When prepping your chayote, you'll notice there's one big seed in the middle, which you simply remove when you slice it in half. If you cannot find chayote, you can use zucchini or another summer squash.*

FRENCH TOAST WITH FOREST BERRIES AND SAUSAGE

 **MAKES 4 SERVINGS**

ONE OF THE FIRST THINGS I ever learned to make was French toast, thanks to the summers I spent at camp as a kid. Every year we'd do an overnight trip, where we'd hike out into the wilderness to look for these beautiful natural waterslides and hidden swimming holes. We'd pack all our food with us and, while the menu would certainly fluctuate, the one constant was the fragrant vanilla French toast the counselors would make while we scoured the grounds for blackberries and salmonberries to scatter on top. One of the counselors finally showed me how to make the French toast, and it's been a breakfast staple ever since. Today I have a few little upgrades that make the adult camper in me pretty happy: I put a little bourbon in the batter and love to use a good, thick sliced bread instead of sandwich bread.

1 pound fresh berries, such as blueberries, blackberries, raspberries

¾ cup sugar

¼ cup freshly squeezed lemon juice

2 cups unsweetened plain almond milk, cold

¼ cup Follow Your Heart vegan egg

1 tablespoon ground cinnamon

1 tablespoon pure vanilla extract

¼ cup bourbon or whiskey

½ teaspoon ground cloves

½ teaspoon ground nutmeg

¼ cup pure maple syrup

4 links Smoked Potato and Artichoke Sausage (page 40) or Field Roast Breakfast Apple Maple Sausage

1 tablespoon safflower oil

6 thick slices vegan bread

3 tablespoons vegan butter

1. In a large bowl, combine the berries, ½ cup of the sugar, and the lemon juice and toss to coat. Set this aside for at least an hour; the berries will start to macerate and will have a nice syrup. Toss again before serving.

2. In a blender, combine the milk, vegan egg, remaining ¼ cup of sugar, and the cinnamon, vanilla, bourbon, cloves, nutmeg, and maple syrup and blend well.

3. Heat a skillet over medium-high heat. Brush the sausages with safflower oil and sauté for 3 minutes on each side, or until heated throughout. Remove from the heat and cover to keep warm.

4. Pour the milk mixture into a shallow pie or baking dish. Dip the bread slices into the liquid, and allow it to soak in. Flip the slice over and repeat, so the bread is thoroughly soaked but not falling apart. On a griddle or in a skillet over medium-high heat, melt a small pat of the butter, then add as many soaked bread slices as will fit onto the griddle. Flip each slice after about 4 minutes, when the first side is golden brown. Cook for another 3 to 4 minutes, until the other side is golden brown. Transfer to a plate and serve with the berries and sausage.

SANDWICHES

BISTRO BURGER

W HEN I LIVED IN the Queen Anne neighborhood of Seattle, there was a little café up the street from my place that made a killer stuffed burger. When I'd stroll in for a happy hour drink, there was a good chance they'd already be sold out: clearly I wasn't the only one who'd made the discovery. So once we perfected our juicy, grillable stuffed Field Roast burger, I knew how we could take it even one step further: by layering local chanterelle mushrooms, roasted tomatoes and a creamy herbed mayo on top. It's become the burger I most crave, and I feel quite certain that your search for the ultimate, deluxe burger can end now.

1 pound chanterelle mushrooms

2 Roma tomatoes, cut into ¼-inch slices

¼ cup safflower oil

2 cloves garlic, minced

Sea salt

Freshly ground black pepper

½ cup vegan mayo

2 sprigs dill, minced

4 sprigs thyme

4 patties Pepper-Stuffed Burgers (page 49) or Field Roast FieldBurgers

4 vegan rustic hamburger buns

2 ounces baby arugula

1. Preheat the oven to 200°F.

2. Clean and slice the chanterelles, removing and discarding any tough stem parts.

3. Toss the tomatoes in 1 tablespoon of the oil and the garlic, and season to taste with salt and pepper. Arrange on a parchment paper–lined baking sheet and heat in the oven for 2 to 3 hours, or until most of the moisture is gone.

4. In a bowl, combine the vegan mayo and dill and set aside.

5. In a skillet over medium heat, heat the remaining 3 tablespoons of oil and add the chanterelles and thyme. Season with salt and pepper.

6. Cook until the mushrooms are soft and slightly browned. Remove from the heat and discard thyme.

7. Grill the burgers, flipping once, about 4 minutes per side, then remove from the heat.

8. Place each burger on a bun. Dress with the dill mayo, mushrooms, tomato slices, and arugula.

MUFFULETTA SANDWICH

PEOPLE HAVE STRONG OPINIONS about what makes a real muffuletta sandwich—a New Orleans staple. Is it the perfect combination of cured meats? Maybe it's the crusty bread? In my mind, it's the olives and giardiniera, that wonderful mélange of tangy pickled vegetables that help to set it apart from your average deli sandwich. While visiting a good friend in New Orleans years ago, I picked up a few tips that help take a good muffuletta to the next level: take some sauce from the tapenade and let it soak into both sides of the bread—you really need some of that briny flavor to cut through the richness of the cold cuts and cheese. And don't stress too much about finding the perfect muffuletta roll. Find a good crusty French roll that's nice and soft on the inside, and you'll be in business.

½ cup kalamata olives, pitted

½ cup pimiento-stuffed green olives

1 tablespoon capers

2 sprigs flat-leaf parsley

2 sprigs oregano

½ cup giardiniera, drained

1 tablespoon red wine vinegar

¼ cup olive oil

2 cloves garlic

4 vegan muffuletta or crusty French rolls

½ pound Mushroom and Herb Roast (page 24), thinly sliced, or Field Roast Wild Mushroom Deli Slices

½ pound Pastrami Roast (page 30), thinly sliced, or Field Roast Smoked Tomato Deli Slices

8 slices Field Roast Creamy Original Chao Cheese Slices

1. Combine the olives, capers, herbs, giardiniera, vinegar, oil, and garlic in a food processor. Pulse until the pieces are reduced consistently to around ⅛ inch.

2. Slice the rolls in half and spread the olive mixture on both sides of each roll.

3. Layer the sliced meats and cheese over one side of each roll.

4. Top the sandwiches with second side and slice into halves.

SERVING SUGGESTIONS: *Serve with kettle-cooked potato chips and a pickle.*

CORNMEAL-CRUSTED OYSTER MUSHROOM PO'BOY

A BAR IN SEATTLE SERVES a bunch of different late-night po'boy sandwiches, which I always thought was a great idea in theory, but sadly its vegan tofu version isn't all that good. Every time I order it, I remind myself that it should really be the last time and I spend the rest of the evening obsessing over how it could be better. So, I decided to walk the walk, making a great vegan version that's a play on the classic New Orleans–style oyster po'boy. The main difference, of course, is that I call for oyster mushrooms instead of oysters.

2 teaspoons white vinegar

1 tablespoon prepared horseradish

½ cup vegan mayo

2 teaspoons smoked paprika

Leaves from 3 sprigs oregano

4 teaspoons freshly squeezed lemon juice

3 cornichons, minced

1 teaspoon freshly ground black pepper

6 cups safflower or another high-heat oil, such as canola, peanut, or vegetable, for frying

1 cup all-purpose flour

½ cup cornmeal

2 tablespoons Follow Your Heart vegan egg

2 teaspoons dried thyme

1 tablespoon onion powder

2 teaspoons garlic powder

2 teaspoons sea salt

1½ cups unsweetened plain almond milk

½ pound oyster mushrooms, lightly brushed clean, divided at the base of the stem with heads and stems left connected and intact, creating pieces or clumps that are 2 inches long and about ½ inch wide

5 vegan, crusty French bread rolls

½ head romaine lettuce, thinly shredded, washed, and spun dry

2 on-the-vine tomatoes, sliced

12 pickles or pickle chips

1 jalapeño pepper, sliced into rings

1. In the food processor, combine the vinegar, horseradish, mayo, paprika, oregano, lemon juice, cornichons, and pepper. Puree until smooth.

2. Heat the oil to 350°F in a deep fryer or heavy Dutch oven. The oil should be at least 2 inches deep.

3. In a bowl, combine the flour, cornmeal, vegan egg, thyme, onion powder, garlic powder, and salt and whisk well. Add the milk and whisk until smooth. Dip the mushroom pieces into the mixture and thoroughly coat, allow the excess to drip off, and fry for 5 to 7 minutes, or until golden brown. Transfer to a paper towel–lined plate.

4. Lightly toast the rolls. Spread a liberal amount of the sauce on each roll, then stuff with lettuce, tomato, pickles, jalapeño, and finally the fried mushrooms. Drizzle with additional sauce.

CHEF'S NOTE: *You're going to want to break out the deep fryer for these, as the crisp cornmeal crust on the mushrooms really relies on it.*

TORTA AHOGADA, PAGE 74

TORTA AHOGADA

ORTA AHOGADA IS A COMMON staple with street vendors in Mexico and taco trucks here on the West Coast. *Ahogada* literally means "drenched" or "drowned." It's no secret that the magic lies in the rich chili sauce, and there are a handful of different ways to approach re-creating it at home. I've taken some cues from my chef friend Dennis Horton, who lives in Los Angeles and knows one or two things about a good Mexican sandwich. He turned me on to a sauce that's similar to the one here, made with pumpkin and sesame seeds along with chile de árbol to give it rich layers of flavor and an intense earthiness. Think mole—with a twist. To prepare the sandwich, you drench the bread in the sauce to let it soak up all that great flavor, grill it, and top it with any taco fixings you like. My go-to is our grilled chili-spiced sausage paired with creamy avocado, crisp red onion, and fresh cilantro.

⅓ cup pumpkin seeds

2 tablespoons sesame seeds

½ teaspoon ground allspice

1 tablespoon dried oregano

1 tablespoon ground cumin

1 teaspoon ground cloves

3 dried chiles de árbol

1 tablespoon sea salt

2 cloves garlic

1½ cups water, plus more if needed

⅔ cup cider vinegar

4 links Oaxacan Chili-Spiced Sausage (page 42) or Field Roast Mexican Chipotle Sausage, sliced lengthwise and brushed with safflower oil

4 crusty sandwich rolls

½ red onion, thinly sliced

1 avocado, peeled, pitted, and sliced

½ bunch cilantro, large stems removed, roughly chopped

1. Preheat the oven to 350°F.

2. Lightly toast the pumpkin seeds on a dry baking sheet in the oven, 5 to 10 minutes.

3. In a blender, combine the seeds, spices, and garlic with the water and vinegar. Blend until smooth, adding water until it has the consistency of a salad dressing.

4. Grill the sausages or cook in a skillet over medium-high heat for 3 to 4 minutes per side. Remove from the heat.

5. Quickly dip both sides of each sandwich roll in the sauce and toast in a skillet or on a grill.

6. Top the rolls with sausage, onion, avocado, and cilantro. Drizzle with extra sauce.

SOUTHWEST PHILLY CHEESESTEAK

 **MAKES 4 SERVINGS**

A GREAT GAME DAY RECIPE or my go-to when having a big, casual gathering at home, this sandwich is made with thinly-sliced Mushroom and Herb Roast (page 24) and a generous layer of chipotle mayonnaise. And of course, any good Philly sandwich wouldn't have much clout without super melty cheese. Here I use our Tomato Chao Slices, but any vegan cheese slice will do the trick: just be sure it melts well, and you'll be in business. When picking up ingredients for the sandwiches, look for a crusty French roll, not a hard-sided baguette—you want something nice and soft and easy to bite through. At the last minute, I'll often decide to double the chipotle mayonnaise recipe because it's such a great condiment on hot dogs or hamburgers, and a nice dip for fresh veggies.

½ cup vegan mayo

1 chipotle pepper in adobo

1 tablespoon freshly squeezed lime juice

1 tablespoon safflower oil

1 yellow onion, sliced into half-moons

¼ pound cremini mushrooms, sliced

1 green bell pepper, sliced into strips

1 jalapeño pepper, sliced into rings

4 cloves garlic, minced

1 tablespoon sea salt

1 loaf vegan crusty French bread, cut into 4 sandwich-size pieces and slit down one side

½ pound Mushroom and Herb Roast (page 24) or Field Roast Celebration Roast, sliced as thinly as possible

8 slices Tomato Cayenne Chao Cheese

4 sprigs cilantro, roughly chopped

1. In a food processor or blender, combine the mayo with the chipotle pepper and lime juice. Set aside.

2. In a skillet over medium-high heat, heat the oil, then add the onion, mushrooms, peppers, garlic, and salt. Sauté for 15 to 20 minutes, stirring occasionally, until the onion is soft and starting to brown on the edges. Lower the heat to medium. Spread the vegetables evenly across the skillet and layer the sliced roast on top, followed by the Chao Cheese. Cook, covered, for 3 to 4 minutes.

3. Toast each piece of bread, spread the mayo mixture on the inside of each roll, and then fill with meat, cheese, and vegetables. Garnish each sandwich with cilantro and serve.

CHEF'S NOTE: *The bread for this sandwich should be soft and pillowy on the inside, crusty and flaky on the outside. Most artisan baguettes have too firm a crust, so look for something softer.*

SMOKY BANH MI

W E HAVE WHAT MUST BE hundreds of Vietnamese restaurants in Seattle, so it's never a challenge to find a good banh mi sandwich. When I first started picking them up for lunch many years ago, they were only two dollars and always wrapped in that characteristic white paper with a rubber band around each one. A banh mi is great with any meat, but we often use our sliced Lemongrass and Ginger Roast (page 18), and beyond that, you'll need a good crusty French roll that's soft in the middle, fresh herbs, and a few quick-pickled vegetables. While it's tempting to go big with this recipe, do keep in mind that these sandwiches are really best enjoyed the same day they're made.

1 tablespoon sesame oil

½ cup soy sauce or tamari

2 tablespoons light brown sugar

4 tablespoons seasoned rice vinegar

2 teaspoons roasted chili paste

2 teaspoons tomato paste

1 clove garlic, minced

1 medium-size carrot, peeled and shredded

1 (2-inch long) piece daikon radish, peeled and shredded

1 tablespoon safflower oil

½ pound Lemongrass and Ginger Roast (page 18) or Field Roast Celebration Roast, sliced into ½-inch-thick steaks

1 loaf vegan crusty French bread, cut into 4 sandwich-size pieces and sliced down one side

⅓ cup vegan mayo

1 small cucumber, peeled and cut into strips about the size of a French fry

1 jalapeño pepper, membrane and seeds removed, cut into strips

8 sprigs cilantro, trimmed at the base

1. In a small saucepan over medium heat, whisk together the sesame oil, ½ cup soy sauce or tamari, brown sugar, 2 tablespoons of the vinegar, and the chili paste, tomato paste, and garlic. Bring to a low boil, then lower the heat to low and let simmer for 10 minutes. Remove the sauce from the heat and set aside.

2. In a medium-size bowl, combine the carrot, daikon, and remaining 2 tablespoons of vinegar, toss thoroughly, and set aside.

3. Brush the steaks with the oil. In a skillet or grill over medium-high heat, grill each steak for 3 minutes per side. Remove the steaks from the heat and cut each into strips. Toss the strips in the sauce, and return to the grill or skillet for another 2 to 3 minutes. Remove from the heat.

4. Lightly toast each piece of bread. Spread the mayo on the inside of each piece of bread, then layer on the roast, cucumber, carrot mixture, jalapeño, and cilantro.

CHEF'S NOTE: *Just as for the Southwest Philly Cheesesteak (page 75), the bread for this sandwich should be soft and pillowy on the inside, crusty and flaky on the outside. Most artisan baguettes have too firm a crust, so look for something a little softer.*

BURNT ENDS BISCUIT SANDWICH

I'VE SPENT A GOOD BIT OF time in Texas and have visited my fair share of barbecue joints, and the deal there is the slow-cooked brisket. A lot of people come just for that brisket. When the pit masters get to the end of the roast, they often make a biscuit sandwich from the leftover pieces, and this recipe is an homage to that. Here I take our Pastrami Roast (page 30), which has that great smoky flavor, and slowly grill it, topping it with a simple slaw and sandwiching it in between a flaky biscuit. It's hard-core vegan BBQ done the real Texas way, without spending 12 hours manning the pit.

---

1 medium-size yellow onion, sliced into ½-inch-thick rounds kept whole like an onion steak

1 tablespoon safflower oil

1 teaspoon sea salt

1 teaspoon freshly ground black pepper

1 pound Pastrami Roast (page 30), sliced into 4 (½-inch-thick) steaks, or Field Roast Smoked Tomato Deli Slices

1½ cups The Sauce BBQ Sauce (page 194), plus more for serving

4 Genesee Biscuits (page 201), sliced in half

1⅓ cups Citrus and Chili Slaw (page 131)

---

1. Start a fire in a wood or charcoal-fired grill and create enough hot coals to last for 45 minutes to 1 hour of cooking. Set your coals up to the side of the grill so there is space to cook without the food getting too hot.

2. Brush the onion steaks with oil on one side and season with salt and pepper. Place, oiled side down, on the grill, and place one pastrami steak on top of each. Baste these with the sauce, using a mop or squirt bottle. Close the grill. After 15 minutes, baste again and flip each steak. Close the grill. After 10 minutes, flip the steak again so that the onion is on the bottom and baste with sauce again. Close the lid. Continue to cook, basting occasionally, until the onion is soft throughout. Move all the steaks to a large cutting board and roughly chop. Baste with more sauce.

3. Arrange the steaks on the lower half of each biscuit, and top each with slaw and the other half of the biscuit.

CHEF'S NOTE: *As an alternative to grilling, in a pinch this dish can be cooked in a skillet over medium-low heat, although you will lose some of the delicious smoky flavor and crispy barbecued edges.*

ISLAND CRUNCH WRAP

IN THE MIDDLE OF WINTER WHEN I start to miss the warm breezes of summer something fierce, these island-style wraps are an easy (albeit temporary) salve. They're made with really simple, fresh ingredients and an Avocado Ranch Dressing (page 198) that we're all addicted to at Field Roast. The mango salsa is something I'll often double, so I end up having leftovers to snack on for the remainder of the week. An easy, portable lunch—you can also simply leave out the tortilla and turn it into a salad instead.

---

1 mango, peeled, pitted, and ¼-inch diced

½ small sweet onion, ¼-inch diced

Leaves from 4 sprigs cilantro, roughly chopped

1 clove garlic, minced

1 Roma tomato, ¼-inch diced

1 small jalapeño pepper, membrane and seeds removed, minced

3 tablespoons freshly squeezed lime juice

1 teaspoon sea salt

½ head green leaf lettuce, shredded into ½-inch pieces, washed, and spun dry

¼ head red cabbage, shredded as thinly as possible

¼ cup Avocado Ranch Dressing (page 198)

4 vegan wraps or burrito-size tortillas

8 pieces Island-Style Coconut Dippers (page 32)

---

1. In a medium-size bowl, combine the mango, onion, cilantro, garlic, tomato, jalapeño, lime juice, and salt. Stir well and set aside.

2. In a large bowl, toss the lettuce, cabbage, and Avocado Ranch to fully combine.

3. To assemble the wraps, lightly warm each tortilla in a microwave or warm oven for about 20 seconds, or until pliable. On each wrap, place a small handful of lettuce mixture, two pieces of Island Coconut Dippers, and a spoonful of mango salsa. Roll up and serve.

SAUSAGE SAN GENNARO

THE FEAST OF SAN GENNARO IN New York City's Little Italy celebrates the traditions of the early Italian immigrants who called the area home. It's a vibrant street festival that's grown over the past eighty years to include street performers, great music, and—of course—authentic Italian food. Now if you ask me, if you're going to get lunch at the festival, it's all about the sausage and peppers, so we were thrilled to get a call a few years back by a restaurant that wanted to sell our Field Roast sausages on site each year. This recipe is our vegan version of that coveted Italian sandwich—a game day favorite around our house, and an easy solution to the inevitable "what's for dinner?" question.

---

2 tablespoons safflower oil

3 cloves garlic, minced

1 red bell pepper, sliced

2 green bell peppers, sliced

1 yellow onion, sliced

2 teaspoons fennel seeds

1 teaspoon sea salt

1 teaspoon red pepper flakes

6 links Fennel and Garlic Sausage (page 38) or Field Roast Italian Sausage, brushed with oil

6 vegan crusty sausage rolls, sliced down the middle with one side left attached

¼ cup stone-ground mustard

---

1. In a skillet over medium heat, heat the safflower oil and add the garlic. Once the garlic has become fragrant, add the bell peppers, onion, fennel seeds, salt, and red pepper flakes. Stirring regularly, sauté until the vegetables have begun to soften and to brown on the edges. Lower the heat to low to keep warm.

2. On a grill over high heat, grill the sausages for about 6 minutes each, or until heated throughout. Grill each roll for about 30 seconds to soften it.

3. Place each sausage in a roll and top with the pepper mixture. Serve with the mustard.

PASTRAMI ON RYE

EVERY NEW YEAR'S DAY, my parents would have friends over to watch the football games—yes, "games": we'd have a number of TVs going at the same time, so regardless of who you were rooting for, you could come over to our place and cheer on your team. Sports differences aside, pastrami sandwiches on rye were always the great equalizer. My dad would pick up corned beef and make a horseradish mayonnaise that was admittedly pretty heavy on the horseradish—and everyone loved them. If you've spent any time in New York delis, you know pastrami sandwiches are often served with Dijon mustard and a pickle on the side, so my version joins both of my favorite traditions: my dad's classic version with the famous deli sandwiches from NYC. The best of both worlds.

½ cup vegan mayo

¼ cup prepared horseradish

1 pound Pastrami Roast (page 30) or Field Roast Wild Mushroom Quarter Loaf, thinly sliced so it is almost beginning to shred

4 slices Creamy Original Field Roast Chao Cheese

8 slices vegan rye bread, lightly toasted

6 large leaves green leaf lettuce, washed and spun dry

2 on-the-vine tomatoes, sliced ¼ inch thick

½ medium-size red onion, thinly sliced

4 dill pickles

¼ cup Dijon mustard

1. In a bowl, combine the mayo and horseradish and set aside.

2. In a skillet over medium heat, place the roast and ¼ cup of water. Lay the slices of Chao Cheese over the top, and cook, covered, for 2 to 3 minutes, until the roast is hot and the cheese is melted. Remove from the heat.

3. Spread the mayo mixture on one side of all eight slices of rye. Top four of the slices with equal amounts of the roast and cheese. Garnish with the lettuce, tomato, and onion and top with the remaining slices of bread, mayo side down.

4. Slice the sandwiches in half and serve with pickles and Dijon.

SOUPS

KHAO SOI

O RIGINALLY FROM NORTHERN THAILAND, khao soi is a hearty, curry-based soup traditionally made with chicken and lots of noodles. While it may seem like there are a lot of ingredients for a very complex recipe, the method is pretty straightforward: make a curry paste and cook
down some onions in a wok, throw in the curry and a little stock, add the coconut milk, noodles,
and our roast instead of the chicken. Then comes the fun part: the garnishes. There are crispy fried
noodles, sliced shallot, pickled mustard greens, lime, and bean sprouts—all really colorful and full
of flavor. See the photo on page 86. For that reason, whenever I'm in a cooking rut, I turn to this khao
soi. If you're not familiar with makrut limes (also known as kaffir limes), they're ugly and dimply
and different from average limes in that they're much more complex and floral. The limes themselves are a little tough to find, but the leaves should be readily available in an Asian market or well-
stocked grocery store; look for them next to the packaged fresh herbs.

3 tablespoons safflower oil

Seeds of 1 cardamom pod

1 (1-inch piece) fresh turmeric, rinsed

1 (1-inch piece) fresh galangal, peeled and
    sliced into coins

3 makrut lime leaves

8 to 10 curry leaves

1 tablespoon coriander seeds

3 cloves garlic, peeled and left whole

1 (4-inch) piece lemongrass stalk, pounded
    with the back of a chef's knife (see
    page 9)

6 dried chiles de árbol or fresh Thai chilis,
    stems removed

¼ cup tamari

2½ cups Lemongrass and Ginger Stock
    (page 195) or vegan vegetable stock

1 medium-size yellow onion, sliced

2 teaspoons sea salt

1 tablespoon sugar

1 (15-ounce) can coconut milk

½ cup safflower or another high-heat oil,
    such as canola, peanut, or vegetable,
    for frying

8 ounces fresh flat vegan Chinese noodles

1 pound Lemongrass and Ginger Roast
    (page 18) or Field Roast Lentil Sage
    Quarter Loaf, cut into ¼-inch strips

1 medium-size shallot, thinly sliced

2 limes, cut into wedges

6 sprigs cilantro

1 cup bean sprouts

½ cup Pickled Mustard Greens (page 128),
    roughly chopped

1. In a small pan or skillet over low heat, heat 1 tablespoon of the oil and add the cardamom, turmeric,
galangal, lime leaves, curry leaves, coriander seeds, garlic, lemongrass, and chiles. Toast the spices
slowly, stirring occasionally, until they smell toasty and fragrant. Remove from the heat and transfer
to a blender. Add the tamari and ¼ cup of the stock to the blender and blend until smooth. Add up to
an additional ¼ cup of stock, if necessary, to blend. Set aside.

2. In a large pot, bring 12 cups of water to a low boil.

3. In a skillet over medium-high heat, heat the remaining oil and add the onion. Sauté, stirring, for 2 to 3 minutes. Then, add the curry mixture from the blender. Allow this to cook down, stirring every 30 seconds or so, for the next 7 minutes. Lower the heat to a low simmer. If the mixture becomes dry, add up to ¼ cup of stock. Allow the mixture to slowly simmer for another 5 minutes.

4. Add the salt, sugar, and remaining stock and increase the heat to high. While stirring, taste for salt and sugar and add more, if desired. Once the liquid has come to a boil, lower the heat to medium and add the coconut milk. Stir to combine and allow to simmer while you are cooking the noodles.

5. In a small saucepan over medium-high heat, heat the frying oil. After about 4 minutes, the oil will be hot. Add a small handful of the fresh noodles and fry them for 2 to 3 minutes, or until they are crispy. Transfer to a paper towel–lined plate.

6. Add the remaining noodles to the pot of boiling water and cook for 3 to 4 minutes; they should still be a little firm. Skim or strain the noodles out of the water and add, along with the roast, to the skillet of curry liquid. Stir to combine the mixture and divide equally among bowls. Garnish each bowl with some crispy noodles, shallot, lime slices, cilantro, sprouts, and greens.

CHEF'S NOTE: *You can use store-bought curry paste here if you don't have time to make your own, but the flavor won't be quite the same. And don't be alarmed at the color of the paste you make at home: it will be a deep, rich orange color because of the turmeric, but once you add it to the soup, it'll mellow out into a nice shade of yellow.*

KHAO SOI, PAGE 84

JACKSON STREET FIVE-ALARM CHILI

 **MAKES 8 SERVINGS**

ONE OF THE MANUFACTURING BUSINESSES down the road from our offices a few summers ago had a chili cook-off, and encouraged us to enter. Now to be clear: this was a group of ardent meat eaters, but we were convinced we could bring a vegan chili that would win over the crowd—and even better, that they wouldn't even know it was vegan. I set out to develop this spicy, rich chili using fresh peppers, sweet potato, and our spicy sausage and it was a hit: they loved it. The secret here lies in not simply relying on chili powder for flavor, but in cooking with fresh pasilla and habañero peppers, which are so much easier to come by now than when I first started cooking years ago. A great warming winter recipe, but also most welcome in the summer atop chili dogs or chili burgers.

½ cup safflower oil

1 yellow onion, cut into ½-inch pieces

1 carrot, peeled and cut into ½-inch pieces

1 red bell pepper, cut into ½-inch pieces

2 tablespoons ground cumin

2 tablespoons chili powder

2 habañero peppers

1 pasilla chile

6 cloves garlic, peeled and left whole

¾ pound Oaxacan Chili-Spiced Sausage (page 42) or Field Roast Mexican Chipotle Sausage, crumbled

1 large yam, peeled and cut into ½-inch pieces

1 tablespoon sea salt

1 (15-ounce) can black beans, drained and rinsed

1 (15-ounce) can pinto beans, drained and rinsed

1 (15-ounce) can crushed tomatoes

1 (15-ounce) can diced tomatoes

3 cups vegan vegetable stock

2 tablespoons balsamic vinegar

1. Preheat the oven to 450°F. In a stockpot over medium heat, heat 2 tablespoons of the oil and add the onion, carrot, bell pepper, cumin, and chili powder. Let cook until the vegetables begin to soften.

2. Toss the habañeros and pasilla with 2 tablespoons of the oil and the garlic cloves and roast in the oven for 15 to 20 minutes, or until the garlic is fully roasted. Remove from the oven, and roughly chop before adding to the vegetables in the stockpot.

3. Add the sausage to the pot and lower the heat to medium-low. Stir occasionally to prevent sticking.

4. Toss the yam in the remaining 4 tablespoons of the oil and 1 teaspoon of the salt, place on a sheet pan, and roast in the oven for 30 minutes, or until soft.

5. Add the beans, tomatoes, stock, vinegar, and remaining 3 teaspoons of salt to the pot and increase the heat to medium. Allow the chili to simmer for 20 minutes, stirring occasionally.

6. Add the roasted yam to the soup and season to taste with salt before serving.

MUSHROOM BURGUNDY STEW

WHEN BRAISED WITH WINE and vegetables, our Mushroom and Herb Roast (page 24), makes one very fine stew. Much of the cook time is inactive, so this is a great recipe for busy families as it tends to make itself at a certain point. While I usually serve this with good crusty bread and a nice glass of dry red wine, it's also great spooned on top of noodles for a hearty, cold weather meal.

¼ cup olive oil

¾ pound cremini mushrooms, cleaned and thickly sliced

3 sprigs thyme

2 teaspoons sea salt

¾ pound Mushroom and Herb Roast (page 24) or Field Roast Wild Mushroom Quarter Loaf, cut on the bias into ½-inch chunks

2 carrots, sliced into ½-inch rounds

1 yellow onion, cut into ½-inch pieces

3 tablespoons vegan butter

3 cloves garlic

2 tablespoons all-purpose flour

½ bottle dry, full-bodied red wine

2 cups Mushroom and Herb Stock (page 196) or vegan mushroom stock

2 bay leaves

1 teaspoon freshly ground black pepper

2 tablespoons tomato paste

¾ cup pearl onions, frozen or fresh, peeled

1. Preheat the oven to 250°F. In a Dutch oven over medium-high heat, heat the oil and add the mushrooms, thyme, and 1 teaspoon of the salt. Stirring occasionally, allow the mushrooms to brown (you should begin to see some bits sticking to the bottom of the pan).

2. After about 7 minutes, add the roast or loaf and lower the heat to medium. Let cook for 2 to 3 minutes, stirring occasionally, then add the carrots and yellow onion and stir to combine. Cook, stirring occasionally, for another 6 or 7 minutes, until the onion starts to become translucent on the edges. At this point, transfer all the contents of the Dutch oven to a heat-safe container and return the pan to the heat. Lower the heat to low and add the butter and garlic. Stir with a wooden spoon while scraping the bottom of the pan to loosen any remaining bits that have stuck.

3. Add the flour to the pan and stir constantly but not vigorously for 3 to 4 minutes, until fully combined and the flour mixture begins to stick to the bottom of the pan.

4. Return the vegetable mixture to the pan and add the wine, mushroom stock, bay leaves, pepper, remaining salt, and tomato paste. Increase the heat to medium and stir to combine the ingredients. After 5 minutes, add the pearl onions, cover, and roast in the oven for 45 minutes.

CHEF'S NOTE: *If you don't have a Dutch oven, you can make this stew in a slow cooker. The only tweak you'll need to make is in cook time: you'll want to set your slow cooker on* high *and double the cook time.*

POSOLE VERDE

O N A TRIP TO LA PAZ with my girlfriend, I came home with an unexpected and most memorable souvenir: the recipe for this authentic posole verde. Our favorite way to get to know a new place when traveling is through the local food, and on our last day there, we stumbled across an unassuming restaurant with the most incredible steaming bowls of green posole. The waiter shared the method and ingredients with me, so back home I set out to make a vegan version that truly lives up to the original. If you're new to posole, you should know that it's all about the accompaniments so we do it up with cilantro, pumpkin seeds, lime, and shredded cabbage. And just like that, I'm transported back to that sleepy beach town and the little hole-in-the-wall restaurant that taught me how to pull off one of the best things I've ever eaten.

1 jalapeño pepper

2 poblano peppers

12 fresh tomatillos or 1 (29-ounce) can, peeled and washed

3 tablespoons safflower oil

1 tablespoon sea salt

6 cups Lemongrass and Ginger Stock (page 195) or vegan vegetable stock

3 cloves garlic, minced

1 tablespoon ground cumin

1 tablespoon chili powder

1 medium-size yellow onion, ¼-inch diced

1 teaspoon sugar

1 (29-ounce) can hominy

12 ounces Lemongrass and Ginger Roast (page 18) or Field Roast Lentil Sage Quarter Loaf, cut into ¼-inch strips

½ cup pumpkin seeds

¼ head cabbage, shredded

4 green onions

8 sprigs cilantro, large stems removed, roughly chopped

2 limes, quartered

1. Over a grill or burner or in a skillet, char the outside skin of the jalapeño and poblano peppers. Transfer them to a clean paper or plastic bag and roll the top closed. Let sit for 15 minutes. Remove the peppers from the bag and peel away the skin. Remove the seeds and stem, and dice the peppers; set aside.

2. Preheat the oven to 450°F.

3. Toss the tomatillos in 1 tablespoon of the oil and 1 teaspoon of the salt, and transfer to a baking dish or baking sheet. Roast in the oven for 10 to 15 minutes, until the tomatillos begin to brown on the skin. Combine the tomatillos and 1 cup of the stock in a blender or food processor and process until smooth.

4. In a pot over medium heat, heat the remaining 2 tablespoons of oil and add the garlic, cumin, and chili powder. Sauté, stirring frequently, for 2 to 3 minutes, until the spices have become fragrant. Add

the yellow onion, sugar, and remaining 2 teaspoons of salt, and sauté for another 10 to 15 minutes, until the onion is translucent.

5. Add the remaining 5 cups of stock and the tomatillo mixture, hominy, and diced peppers. Stir to combine. Increase the heat to medium-high. Stirring occasionally, allow the soup to come to a boil. Lower the heat to medium-low, and simmer for 35 to 40 minutes.

6. Add the roast or loaf and stir to combine. Allow the soup to simmer for 10 more minutes, then serve with pumpkin seeds, cabbage, green onions, cilantro, and lime wedges to garnish.

ROASTED SUGAR PIE PUMPKIN STEW

Y OU'VE HEARD OF ONE-POT SOUPS? Well, this is actually a zero-pot recipe, as we're doing all the actual cooking inside the pumpkins themselves. This was a favorite at our holiday table last year and for good reason: the house smells warm and fragrant, there's a sense of anticipation as the Peruvian-influenced stew bakes, and you get a lot of "oooh and ahhh" factor when you bring the pumpkins out to the table. To serve, scoop out some of the flesh and stew right into your favorite soup bowls and garnish with a little cilantro and toasted pumpkin seeds. Personally, I love to set out the pumpkins and garnishes and let people serve themselves—it always tends to be a good conversation starter and helps bring together friends who may not have known one another well to begin with.

---

1 yellow onion, ¼-inch diced

2 carrots, peeled and ¼-inch diced

3 stalks celery, ¼-inch diced

⅔ pound purple potatoes, cut into ½-inch pieces

1 teaspoon ground cinnamon

Small pinch of ground cloves

1 tablespoon ground cumin

2 tablespoons chili powder

1 cup quinoa, rinsed

2 teaspoons sea salt

1 apple, peeled, cored, and ½-inch diced

4 cloves garlic, minced

1 jalapeño pepper, ¼-inch diced

¼ cup plus 1 tablespoon olive oil

2 teaspoons freshly ground black pepper

3 sugar pie pumpkins or red kuri squash, tops cut off, seeds and membrane scooped out and discarded

4 cups vegan vegetable stock

2½ cups baby spinach

½ cup toasted pumpkin seeds

5 sprigs cilantro, large stems removed, chopped

---

1. Preheat the oven to 250°F.

2. In a large bowl, combine the onion, carrot, celery, potato, spices, quinoa, salt, apple, garlic, jalapeño, olive oil, and black pepper. Toss well.

3. Fill each pumpkin with the mixture, dividing equally. Pour the vegetable stock into each pumpkin until it reaches ½ inch from the top. Place the top of each pumpkin back on top to cover. Transfer the pumpkins to a baking sheet and bake for about 90 minutes. Liquid will be bubbling out.

4. To serve, place a small handful of spinach in each bowl and scoop out the stew onto the spinach, scraping some of the soft flesh of the pumpkin from the side while scooping. Garnish with pumpkin seeds and cilantro. Keep some extra stock heated while serving. In case soup comes out a little thick, add some stock to thin it out.

CHEF'S NOTE: *If you have a hard time finding sugar pie pumpkins, feel free to use kuri squash instead.*

PEA SOUP WITH CHARRED
SPICY SAUSAGE, PAGE 98

PEA SOUP WITH CHARRED SPICY SAUSAGE

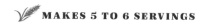 **MAKES 5 TO 6 SERVINGS**

PEA SOUP IS SOMETHING I grew up eating, and it's one of the first soups I learned to make on my own. It's the ultimate in fuss-free cooking. I still make a very basic pot of soup, but it doesn't take too much effort to really dress it up. Black pepper is the most underappreciated ingredient in most pea soup recipes, and I don't shy away from it here. It's a great zippy contrast to earthy, creamy peas. Top each bowl with grilled, sliced Oaxacan Chili-Spiced Sausage (page 42) and caramelized leeks for a most grown-up version of this childhood favorite. See the photo on pages 96–97.

2 tablespoons safflower oil, plus more for grilling the sausage

½ yellow onion, ¼-inch diced

1 carrot, ¼-inch diced

2 stalks celery, ¼-inch diced

3 cloves garlic, minced

3 teaspoons sea salt

2 bay leaves

2 teaspoons chili powder

2 sprigs thyme

1 pound dried split peas, rinsed, any stones or debris removed

8 cups vegan vegetable stock

2 tablespoons olive oil

2 small leeks, cleaned and thinly sliced, after trimming the top at about 1 inch from the tender white part of the leek

Leaves from 2 sprigs tarragon, minced

4 links Oaxacan Chili-Spiced Sausage (page 42) or Field Roast Mexican Chipotle Sausage, sliced or crumbled

1. In a stockpot over medium heat, heat the safflower oil and add the onion, carrot, celery, garlic, and 1 teaspoon of the salt. Allow the veggies to cook, stirring occasionally, for 10 to 15 minutes, or until the onion has become translucent.

2. Add the bay leaves, chili powder, and thyme, and stir. When the mixture becomes fragrant with thyme, add the split peas, stock, and the remaining 2 teaspoons of salt. Stir the mixture, increase the heat to medium-high, and cover. Allow the soup to cook for 15 minutes, stirring occasionally, then lower heat to medium-low. Cook, stirring occasionally, for another 30 to 35 minutes, or until the peas have lost their shape and the soup is smooth. Season to taste with additional salt.

3. While the soup is cooking, in a small skillet over medium heat, heat the olive oil and add the leeks and 1 teaspoon of salt. Sauté this mixture for 5 to 7 minutes, or until the leeks become visibly soft, then lower the heat to low, add the tarragon, and stir. Cook, stirring occasionally, for 20 to 25 minutes, or until the leeks are lightly caramelized. Remove from the heat and set aside.

4. On a grill over medium-high heat, brush the sausages with safflower oil and place directly on the grill. Turn the sausages after 3 to 4 minutes; they are finished when hot throughout, usually another 2 to 3 minutes. For this dish, cook the sausages for an extra minute per side to increase the char, as it provides a nice smoky flavor and texture contrast. Serve the soup topped with the sausage and leeks.

ITALIAN WEDDING SOUP

A SIMPLE, RUSTIC SOUP IS what I so often crave in the cooler months, and Italian Wedding Soup always fits the bill. Traditionally this recipe often calls for meatballs and orzo pasta, but mine relies on pantry staples you may already have on hand with the addition of our Fennel and Garlic Sausage (page 38) and some crisp apple for sweetness. Our Vegan Béchamel (page 192) makes the soup silky and creamy without feeling heavy, but if you want a quick substitution, any plant-based milk will work just fine. Feel free to slice the sausage into small meatball shapes to remain a bit more traditional or crumble it up and use it as more of a ground meat instead. With a nice slice of crusty bread, dinner (or lunch) is served.

---

2 tablespoons safflower oil

6 cloves garlic, minced

1 tablespoon fennel seeds

1 large yellow onion, ¼-inch diced

1 large carrot, peeled and chopped

2 teaspoons red pepper flakes

1 tablespoon dried basil

1 head dinosaur kale, stemmed and roughly chopped

2 Yukon Gold potatoes, peeled and ½-inch diced

2 teaspoons sea salt

7 cups vegan vegetable stock

1 tablespoon vegan butter

1 firm green apple, peeled, cored, and ¼-inch diced

1 cup Vegan Béchamel (page 192) or unsweetened plain almond milk

2 teaspoons freshly ground black pepper

3 links or ⅔ pound Fennel and Garlic Sausage (page 38) or Field Roast Italian Sausage, grilled and cut into ¾-inch slices

---

1. In a stockpot over medium-low heat, heat the oil and then sauté the garlic and fennel seeds for 3 to 4 minutes, or until very fragrant.

2. Add the onion, carrot, red pepper flakes, and basil and increase the heat to medium. Stirring occasionally, allow the vegetables to sauté until the onion is translucent.

3. Add the kale, potato, salt, and stock and increase the heat to medium-high. Cover and, stirring occasionally, allow to cook for about 20 minutes.

4. While the soup is cooking, in a small skillet over medium heat, sauté the apple in the butter until the apple starts to brown, about 10 minutes. Remove from the heat and set aside.

5. Add the remaining ingredients, including the sautéed apples, to the soup, lower the heat to low, and cover. Allow to simmer for about 10 more minutes and serve.

LEEK DUMPLINGS IN DASHI, PAGE 102

LEEK DUMPLINGS IN DASHI

WHILE WE'RE A BIG DUMPLING TOWN, finding great plant-based dumplings can be a challenge. Until now. I crave this recipe when I'm under the weather and am convinced they have healing properties. They're also great for rainy-day lunches and are particularly nice in the spring when leeks are everywhere at the farmers' market. The best part? These addictive little numbers seem far more complex to make than they really are, so they're a great one to pull out to wow friends and family. To get them going, you simply buy wonton wrappers, make a leek filling with our Lemongrass and Ginger Roast (page 18), pull together a savory broth, and steam the dumplings in the broth. The kombu boosts the umami in the broth, making it superfragrant and flavorful.

6 cups Mushroom and Herb Stock
  (page 196) or vegan mushroom stock

1 medium-size piece kombu

2 tablespoons coconut oil

1 medium-size shallot, minced

4 cloves garlic, minced

2 tablespoons minced fresh ginger

4 green onions, sliced

1 medium-size leek, cleaned, tough ends
  removed, sliced

8 ounces Lemongrass and Ginger Roast
  (page 18) or Field Roast Lentil Sage
  Quarter Loaf, ground

2 tablespoons rice vinegar

2 tablespoons tamari

About 24 wonton wrappers

EQUIPMENT

Bamboo steamer

1. In a pot, bring the stock to a boil and add the kombu. Lower the heat to low and cover.

2. In medium-size pan or skillet over medium-high heat, heat the oil and add the shallot, garlic, ginger, green onions, leeks, and roast or loaf. Sauté, stirring occasionally, for 5 minutes. Lower the heat to medium and continue to cook for 5 minutes, stirring occasionally to keep everything from sticking to the bottom of the pan. Add the vinegar and tamari. Lower the heat to low and simmer until the liquid is absorbed fully. Transfer the mixture to a plate and cool in the fridge until it is easy to handle.

3. Fill a ramekin or small bowl with about ½ cup of water and place on a clean board. Lay out a few of the wrappers, and spoon a healthy tablespoon of the filling into each wrapper. Wet your fingers in the bowl and dab around the outside edge of the wrappers. Fold one corner over the filling to the diagonal corner, creating a triangle, and seal the edges with your fingers. Bring the acute-angled edges together and seal them with a little more water from the bowl. Do this until all filling has been used up. Steam in a bamboo steamer for 3 minutes.

4. Place six or so dumplings in each bowl and ladle the broth over the top.

ROASTED CHILI TOMATO BISQUE

WHEN THE CRAVING FOR grilled cheese and tomato soup strikes on a rainy Seattle afternoon, this is the recipe I turn to. Over and over again. A quick, easy soup you can throw together in twenty minutes, it's a nice stand-in for the canned version you may have grown up with. Here, the chili paste, garlic, and ginger add layers of flavor and the coconut milk tempers some of the heat, making this a super creamy soup perfectly poised for sandwich dipping.

2 tablespoons coconut oil

2 tablespoons roasted chili paste

5 cloves garlic, minced

1 stalk fresh lemongrass, pounded with the back of a chef's knife and cut in half (see page 9)

1 (½-inch) piece fresh ginger, peeled and minced

1 tablespoon sugar, or 2 teaspoons agave syrup

1 (28-ounce) can crushed tomatoes

2 (13-ounce) cans coconut milk

⅔ cup soy sauce or tamari

5 sprigs (about two dozen leaves) basil

1 tablespoon sesame oil

1. In a large saucepan over medium-low heat, heat the coconut oil and add the chili paste, garlic, lemongrass, ginger, and sugar. Sauté for 15 minutes, stirring regularly; the mixture should become very fragrant. For a deeper, richer, nuttier flavor, you may continue to sauté for another 10 minutes over low heat, being careful not to burn the mixture.

2. Remove the lemongrass stalks and discard.

3. Add the remaining ingredients and increase the heat to medium. Stirring occasionally, let the soup come up to temperature slowly. After 15 minutes, remove from the heat and use an immersion blender or blender to process until smooth. Then, return to the heat and let simmer for another 5 minutes.

4. Remove from the heat and serve.

SALADS

LARB SALAD

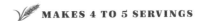

A CLASSIC THAI APPETIZER, this ground meat salad is traditionally made with pork, chicken, or beef and is flavored differently depending on the region. This version uses our crumbled grain meat for the base, curry paste and lime juice for flavor, and salty peanuts for crunch. Scoop it onto lettuce leaves and you're in for a really refreshing, herbaceous, and satisfying snack. This always strikes me as a recipe meant to share, so gather together some of your favorite people to help you dig in. For a larger crowd or for more of a meal, serve with Coconut Rice (page 136) or sticky rice.

¼ cup peanuts

¾ pound Little Saigon Meatloaf (page 44) or Field Roast Classic Meatloaf

¼ cup safflower oil

1 tablespoon minced fresh ginger

4 cloves garlic, minced

½ medium-size shallot, minced

2 tablespoons vegan green curry paste

1 jalapeño pepper, thinly sliced, seeds and membrane removed if sensitive to heat

⅓ bunch cilantro, roughly torn, leaving the leaves whole

4 sprigs mint

2 tablespoons freshly squeezed lime juice

10 lettuce leaves

1. Toast the peanuts in a dry skillet over medium heat and roughly chop.

2. Crumble the meatloaf by hand or pulse in a food processor into pea-size pieces.

3. In a wok or large skillet over medium heat, heat the oil and add the ginger, garlic, and shallot. Cook for 2 to 3 minutes, stirring regularly, until the mixture is fragrant. Add the curry paste while stirring.

4. Once the curry paste is incorporated, add the crumbled meatloaf and jalapeño and increase the heat to medium-high. Cook, stirring regularly, for 3 and 4 minutes.

5. Lower the heat to low and allow to simmer for an additional 3 to 4 minutes.

6. When the mixture is heated thoroughly, remove from the heat and add the fresh herbs and lime juice.

7. Serve with lettuce leaves and garnish with peanuts.

LAOTIAN CITRUS SALAD WITH HERBS

I USED TO LIVE BY A LAOTIAN RESTAURANT that had a pretty well-known karaoke night, and we'd end up spending an entire evening there, drinking good beer and ordering off the menu when hunger would strike (as it's known to do). A lot of the dishes would come out with fresh herbs and lettuces that you'd tear off and use as wraps, so this salad is very much inspired by that culinary tradition. My version uses slices of grapefruit, which add a nice bitterness and brightness that's ultimately balanced by the juicy curry dressing. While it's great as a side dish, this salad can easily graduate into more of a meal by adding a bit of protein—I love using our Island-Style Coconut Dippers (page 32) to lay on top, but you could do a grilled sausage as well.

1 head romaine lettuce, halved lengthwise, chopped into 1-inch pieces, washed, and spun dry

3 ounces mixed greens

⅓ cup Fresh Juiced Curry Dressing (page 197)

3 green onions, green tops sliced very thinly on the bias so they curl

1 grapefruit, cut into supremes (see Chef's Note)

Leaves from 4 large sprigs mint (about 18 leaves)

Leaves from 4 large sprigs basil (about 18 leaves)

½ bunch cilantro, roughly chopped

1 jalapeño pepper, thinly sliced

1 small cucumber, peeled, seeded, and ¼-inch diced

2 carrots, peeled and shredded

⅓ pound daikon radish, peeled and shredded

¼ cup roasted peanuts, roughly chopped

1. In a large mixing bowl, combine the romaine, mixed greens, and dressing. Toss until coated.

2. Arrange the salad on cold plates and garnish with all the remaining ingredients. Use the colors, shapes, and textures to build upward on top of the greens.

3. Finish with the peanuts.

CHEF'S NOTE: Supremes *refers to the insides of the citrus segments whose peel, membrane, and white pith have been cut away. There are many simple tutorials on the Internet, but if you don't feel comfortable with your knife skills, you can always peel the citrus and separate the segments by hand, leaving the membrane intact.*

CUCUMBER SALAD WITH
THAI CHILIS, PAGE 112

CUCUMBER SALAD WITH THAI CHILIS

I GROW CUCUMBERS IN MY GARDEN, and each year there's that inevitable point in the season when we have more cucumbers than we know what to do with. In addition to snacking on them endlessly and giving them away to friends and co-workers, I always turn to this salad—on repeat. It's fresh and crisp and supersimple to pull together, making it a prime candidate for those occasional Seattle evenings when it's too darn hot to cook. There are innumerable cucumber salad recipes, but the complex, building heat from the Thai chilis makes this one truly stand out.

DRESSING

2 cloves garlic, minced

2 teaspoons sweet chili sauce

2 teaspoons sesame oil

2 Thai chilis

½ cup seasoned rice vinegar

VEGETABLES

2 English cucumbers, peeled and cut into ⅛-inch slices

½ red onion, thinly sliced

1 jalapeño or serrano pepper, thinly sliced

½ bunch green onions, thinly sliced on the bias

GARNISH

Leaves from 2 sprigs dill, roughly chopped

½ bunch cilantro, large stems removed, roughly chopped

1. In a food processor or blender, combine the garlic, chili sauce, sesame oil, Thai chilis, and vinegar to make the dressing.

2. In a large bowl, combine the vegetables with the dressing. Allow the salad to marinate for 1 to 2 hours in the fridge.

3. Before serving, toss the salad and garnish with dill and cilantro.

CHEF'S NOTE: *If you're comfortable using a mandoline, really thin cucumber slices make this salad feel even more special, even elegant. Also, if you can't find Thai chilis, serrano peppers will work just fine.*

AUTUMN ROCKET SALAD WITH CHAO CRISPS

 **MAKES 6 SERVINGS**

ARUGULA GROWS LIKE A WEED in Seattle; these days I actually grow it up on my roof. I originally got the seeds from my great-aunt who passed away about a year ago. She was an amazing gardener, and at her memorial, my family shared all these little bags of seeds she'd diligently catalogued over the years. I took home the package reading: "Florence 1994 Arugula." and planted them. I think of her often whenever we clip the leaves to make this salad. Besides having it at the ready most weeks of the year, I love arugula because it has a nice bitterness yet it's still a really tender green. Most people associate it with spring, but this salad has pops of fall, thanks to the butternut squash and cranberries—and of course those unforgettable Chao Cheese crisps. They're great here, but also a big hit on top of burgers or sandwiches.

1 pound butternut squash, peeled, seeded, and ¾-inch diced	2 tablespoons pure maple syrup
1 tablespoon safflower oil	Leaves from 2 sprigs thyme
2 teaspoons sea salt	7 ounces Creamy Original Chao Slices
6 cloves roasted garlic	3 ounces arugula
¼ cup red wine vinegar	1 small head radicchio, leaves torn from stem
¼ cup olive oil	1 small fennel bulb, cored and thinly sliced
1 teaspoon freshly ground black pepper	½ cup dried cranberries

1. Preheat the oven to 425°F.

2. Toss the squash with the safflower oil and 1 teaspoon of the salt. Arrange on a baking sheet and place in the oven. Roast the squash for 20 to 25 minutes, or until it starts to become tender. Depending on your oven, this may need to be stirred halfway through the cooking time. Remove from the heat and set aside.

3. In a blender or food processor, combine the roasted garlic, vinegar, olive oil, remaining teaspoon of salt, pepper, maple syrup, and thyme. Process until smooth.

4. Currently Chao Cheese is only available in slices, but can still be utilized as shreds. Shredding the Chao may be accomplished by chilling the package in the freezer for 20 minutes to firm it up, and using a normal cheese grater or the shredding attachment of a food processor, turning the sides of the slices toward the grater. Alternatively, the cheese may be sliced into thin shards, using a sharp knife and patience.

continues on page 114

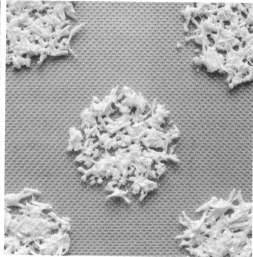

5. On a sheet pan lined with waxed paper or a silicone mat, arrange the Chao shreds into mounded 2-inch circles. Use 2 to 3 tablespoons of cheese for each crisp. Place the sheet pan in the oven and bake for 10 minutes, or until the edges of the Chao circles begin to brown. Remove from the oven and set aside.

6. Toss the arugula, radicchio, and fennel together with half of the dressing, taste, and add more dressing to your liking. Plate the greens and garnish with the Chao crisps and dried cranberries.

CASCADE COBB SALAD

 **MAKES 5 TO 6 SERVINGS**

EVERY YEAR IN THE LATE SUMMER MONTHS, my girlfriend and I head to Lake Chelan in eastern Washington. If you're not familiar with the region, the eastern part of the state is where a lot of our fruit is grown. While you're cycling the quiet, winding roads, you can literally smell the pears ripening in the nearby orchards. I realize pears aren't a traditional inclusion in a Cobb salad, but I love any opportunity to create a Northwest version of a classic dishes, and that's exactly what I did here. The sweet pears, buttery mushrooms, and creamy white beans make for a really memorable, filling salad—one that takes me right back to those fragrant orchards in Chelan and one that I hope will become a new favorite at your kitchen table.

DRESSING

¼ cup cider vinegar

2 teaspoons stone-ground mustard

½ teaspoon agave syrup

Leaves from 1 sprig thyme

½ teaspoon freshly ground black pepper

1 teaspoon sea salt

1 clove black garlic, peeled

3 tablespoons olive oil

SALAD

½ pound chanterelle mushrooms, cleaned, tough parts of stems removed, and roughly chopped

2 tablespoons safflower oil

2 sprigs thyme

1 teaspoon sea salt

2 links Smoked Potato and Artichoke Sausage (page 40) or Field Roast Smoked Apple Sage Sausage, brushed with safflower oil

½ head romaine lettuce, halved lengthwise, chopped into ½-inch pieces, washed, and spun dry

4 leaves kale, stripped from stems, sliced into ½-inch intervals, washed, and spun dry

1½ cups baby arugula

1 pear (Bartlett or Red Anjou), peeled, cored, and ½-inch diced

⅔ cup cooked small white beans

6 slices Coconut Herb Chao Slices, cubed

1. Preheat the oven to 450°F.

2. In a blender, combine all the dressing ingredients, except the oil. Blend at medium speed while drizzling in the olive oil. Set aside.

3. In a bowl, combine the mushrooms, safflower oil, thyme, and sea salt. Toss to coat. Arrange the mushrooms on a baking sheet and roast in the oven for 10 minutes. Remove from the oven and set aside. Discard the thyme sprigs.

4. Cook the sausages in a skillet or grill at medium heat for 6 to 7 minutes, turning halfway through. Transfer the sausages to a cutting board and slice into ¼-inch slices. Set aside to rest at room temperature.

5. Combine all the remaining ingredients with the mushrooms, sausage. and dressing. Toss to coat, and season to taste with salt and pepper.

6. Plate and serve.

CHEF'S NOTE: *If you can't get hold of chanterelles, feel free to use oyster, cremini, or even button mushrooms instead. To clean mushrooms, brush them with a dry brush or paper towel. Black garlic is regular garlic that is slowly heated over a long period of time, allowing it to caramelize, resulting in intense flavor. You can find this at most specialty and Asian grocery stores, but feel free to use regular garlic if you can't track down black garlic.*

SMOKY KALUA JACKFRUIT (PAGE 185), MACARONI
SALAD (PAGE 120), LOMI LOMI SALAD (PAGE 119)

LOMI LOMI SALAD

I'VE VISITED HAWAII a number of times and eating on the island is always one of the high-lights—there are so many fresh ingredients and everything is at the peak of flavor because a lot of it is grown right there. On the way home from a good morning swim, I love stopping at one of the roadside plate lunch spots and getting starchy rice, macaroni salad, and gravy—Hawaiian comfort food at its best. On the island, this salad is usually made with raw marinated salmon chopped up with a few veggies, but here we have our vegan version using my cured Tomato Lox (page 58). It's a supersimple and fresh condiment or accompaniment, and is a great addition to our plant-based Hawaiian Plate Lunch (along with the Smoky Kalua Jackfruit, page 185, and Macaroni Salad, page 120).

½ batch (about 12 ounces) Tomato Lox (page 58)

1 medium-size jalapeño pepper, seeds and membrane removed, minced

2 tablespoons minced yellow onion

2 tablespoons olive oil

2 green onions, thinly sliced

3 sprigs cilantro, large stems removed, chopped

1. Drain the liquid off the lox. Chop the lox until it resembles a rough mince.

2. In a large bowl, combine the minced lox and all the remaining ingredients. Toss until fully coated. Refrigerate for 1 hour before serving.

MACARONI SALAD

Y FAVORITE PART OF THE Hawaiian Plate Lunch (see photo page 118), this is a no-frills, basic macaroni salad. It's not putting on airs or trying to be something it's not. It's pretty darn starchy, and not entirely all that healthy. But it's so damn good. I use vegan mayonnaise here and a basic yellow mustard because that's what I grew up with. There's a little crunch, thanks to the sesame seeds. They are a staple ingredient when you order this at the Hawaiian roadside spots, so I've kept them in my version. After all, why mess with a really, really good thing?

4 teaspoons sea salt	1 teaspoon smoked paprika
1 pound elbow macaroni noodles	1 large carrot, peeled and shredded
1 cup vegan mayo	4 sprigs or ½ bunch green onion, thinly sliced
2 tablespoons white wine vinegar	
2 tablespoons yellow mustard	2 teaspoons sesame seeds

1. Fill a large pot with water, add 3 teaspoons of the salt, and bring to a boil over high heat. Add the macaroni and stir. Cook the noodles for about 5 minutes, stirring occasionally, until they are fully cooked but still have a bite (al dente). Drain the noodles and rinse with cold water; set aside.

2. In a large bowl, combine the mayo, vinegar, mustard, the remaining teaspoon of salt, and the paprika; stir well. Add the noodles (which should be dry), carrot, green onion, and sesame seeds. Stir the mixture until the noodles are fully coated.

GERMAN POTATO SALAD

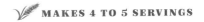

A S A KID, MY FAMILY AND I WOULD visit Pike Place Market on occasion, and the charming shop Bavarian Meats was always a necessary detour. It specializes in homemade sausages and European imports, but the German potato salad was what always got me: served warm with the bite of vinegar and a generous handful of fresh herbs, it's a very far cry from the mayonnaise-laden potato salads so many of us are used to. The red potatoes are key here as they're firm and hold their structure (no one wants a mushy potato salad). Instead of bacon, we use Field Roast Smoked Tomato Deli Slices; if you have trouble finding them, look for your favorite smoky seitan meat product instead.

2 pounds red potatoes	2 tablespoons sugar
5 teaspoons sea salt	⅓ cup cider vinegar
4 ounces Field Roast Smoked Tomato Quarter Loaf or Deli Slices	1 tablespoon Dijon mustard
Safflower or canola oil spray	6 sprigs chives, minced
3 tablespoons safflower oil	Leaves from 3 sprigs parsley, minced
3 cloves garlic, minced	Leaves from 3 sprigs tarragon, roughly chopped
1 large shallot, sliced	1 teaspoon freshly ground black pepper

1. In a large stockpot, combine the potatoes and 1 tablespoon of the salt and cover with water. Cook over medium-high heat for about 25 minutes. The potatoes should be tender and easily pierced by a fork or knife. Remove from the heat, drain, and set aside.

2. Preheat the oven to 400°F. On a parchment paper–lined sheet pan, arrange the Field Roast slices (if using the Quarter Loaf, slice into ⅛-inch-thick slices) and lightly spray with oil. Bake for 5 to 7 minutes. Remove from the oven. The Field Roast will be a little soft, but will become crispy as it cools on the sheet pan. Once cooled, remove the Field Roast from the sheet pan, roughly chop (to resemble coarse bacon bits), and set aside.

3. In a pan over medium-low heat, heat the oil and add the garlic and shallot. Sauté, stirring occasionally, until the shallot has become translucent, about 15 minutes. Lower the heat to low and add the sugar, vinegar, and Dijon. Stir until combined, then remove from heat.

4. Cut the potatoes into ¼-inch slices and place in large bowl. Add the chopped Field Roast, shallot mixture, herbs, pepper, and remaining 1 teaspoon of salt. Toss to combine.

CHILLED ASPARAGUS SALAD WITH HAZELNUTS

WINTER CAN FEEL LONG AND GRAY in Seattle, so when the cherry blossoms start blooming and spring produce begins to grace the market stands, there is a palpable, almost visceral excitement around the city. As the season progresses, we see the big, fat asparagus stalks from Mexico yield to thinner stalks from California, and finally the most tender local Washington asparagus. When tasked with what to do with an enthusiastic haul, I always turn to this simple, chilled salad: a no-fuss celebration of the flavor of asparagus paired with hazelnuts, another local ingredient we love. Because it doesn't require reheating, this recipe is an easy choice for picnics or potlucks—just the thing to get us all looking forward to the even warmer months ahead.

½ cup hazelnuts

2 Meyer lemons

2 teaspoons sea salt

1½ pounds asparagus

¼ cup vegan mayo

Leaves from 4 sprigs tarragon

1 tablespoon stone-ground mustard

2 tablespoons red wine vinegar

Freshly ground black pepper

1. Preheat the oven to 350°F.

2. Toast the hazelnuts in the preheated oven until fragrant. The skins will split and turn dark brown.

3. Slice one lemon in half. On a grill or in a skillet, grill it, flesh side down, over high heat for 5 to 7 minutes, or until there are visible grill marks on the flat side. Set aside.

4. Bring a large pot of water to boil and add all the salt. Prepare an ice bath and set aside.

5. Wash and trim the tough ends from the asparagus. Add the asparagus to the boiling water and blanch for 2 to 3 minutes, when the asparagus is still al dente. Drain the water and transfer the asparagus to the ice bath to cool it and stop it from cooking. Drain the asparagus and set aside.

6. Zest and juice the second lemon.

7. In a blender or food processor, combine the mayo, half of the hazelnuts, and the tarragon, mustard, vinegar, and lemon zest and juice.

8. Toss the asparagus lightly in the dressing and arrange on a plate. Garnish with pepper, the remaining hazelnuts, and the grilled lemon.

MEDITERRANEAN GRILLED SQUASH COUSCOUS SALAD

 **MAKES 6 SERVINGS**

THIS SALAD HAS SUMMER BARBECUE season written all over it, and for good reason: the eggplant and sausage are done on the grill so they get those nice char marks; you'll toss in some fragrant fresh mint and oregano, and whisk up a simple white balsamic dressing. It has a light, Mediterranean vibe—the quintessential outdoor picnic food. While the recipe calls for yellow squash (pattypans are my favorite), you can use any squash or zucchini you like here. No hard and fast rules. That being said, I do try to make the salad a day in advance to allow the flavors a chance to really develop.

4 healthy-size sprigs flat-leaf parsley, large stems removed, leaves minced

2 tablespoons Dijon mustard

⅓ cup olive oil

Leaves from 4 sprigs mint, minced

3 cloves garlic, minced

⅓ cup white balsamic vinegar

4 teaspoons sea salt

Leaves from 4 sprigs oregano, minced

2 cups dried Israeli couscous

2 small yellow squash, sliced into ½-inch rounds

1 medium-size firm eggplant, sliced into ½-inch rounds

2 links Smoked Potato and Artichoke Sausage (page 40) or Field Roast Italian Sausage

1 small red onion, sliced into thin half-moons

1. In a bowl, combine the parsley, Dijon, olive oil, mint, garlic, vinegar, 1 teaspoon of the salt, and the oregano; whisk well.

2. Fill a large pot with water, add the remaining salt, and bring to a boil over high heat.

3. Add the couscous and stir. Cook for 3 to 4 minutes, until the couscous is soft but still has a bite to it (al dente). Strain the couscous and lightly rinse with water. Set aside for another 5 to 6 minutes, to allow the couscous to dry.

4. Pour two thirds of the dressing over the couscous and toss to coat. Set aside.

5. Using the remaining dressing, lightly coat the squash and eggplant. In a skillet, or on a grill, over high heat, grill the sausage, eggplant, and squash. The squash should take 2 to 3 minutes per side; the eggplant, 5 to 6 minutes per side; and the sausage, 3 to 4 minutes per side. When all are fully cooked, slice each piece into bite-size pieces. Cut the sausage into rounds and divide the squash and eggplant into wedges. Add the grilled ingredients to the couscous and onion and toss to combine.

CHEF'S NOTE: *Israeli couscous is easy to overcook, so I like to cook it for just a few minutes until tender and rinse with cold water to stop the cooking process. Then, spread it out on a large plate or small baking sheet so it doesn't all clump together.*

VEGETABLES & SIDES

CÉLERI RÉMOULADE

CELERY ROOT, ALSO KNOWN AS CELERIAC, strikes me as greatly underutilized in American cuisine, and I've always loved its fresh, bright flavor and pleasant crunch. When traveling around France in particular, you'll often see a light celery root salad served alongside bites of terrine or pâté—quite smart as it helps to balance out those heavier, richer flavors. For quite some time, I've wanted to see more of that French tradition on our own table, so I developed this simple recipe featuring shaved celery root cloaked in a lemony mustard dressing with flecks of fresh tarragon. It's light and snappy and can also be served as a side dish or spooned atop your favorite salad.

1 large or 2 small celery root(s), peeled and
    cut into matchsticks

2 tablespoons freshly squeezed lemon juice

1 tablespoon cider vinegar

Leaves from 2 sprigs tarragon, minced

1 teaspoon sea salt

1 tablespoon stone-ground mustard

Pinch of ground white pepper

⅔ cup vegan mayo

1. Toss the celery root with the lemon juice and cider vinegar in a small bowl. Cover and let sit for 30 minutes.

2. Combine the remaining ingredients with the celery root.

3. Cover the bowl, place in the fridge to chill until cold, and serve.

CHEF'S NOTE: *Celery root is available in most well-stocked produce departments. It looks like a big gnarly ball of something that you'd dig out of the earth, but don't be intimidated. Beneath its tough exterior is brilliant, starchy white flesh packed with complex flavor.*

CHARRO BEANS

A TRUE TEX-MEX STAPLE AND ONE OF my favorite side dishes, these beans are classic com-fort food. Traditionally made with bacon and chorizo, I use our Oaxacan Chili-Spiced Sausage (page 42) and Mushroom and Herb Roast instead to make one robust, hearty pot of beans. These go really well with the Cochinita Pibil (page 182), as a filling for tacos or a topping on grain bowls, or as a killer addition to a Mexican breakfast—which I'm always a big fan of on slow, lazy weekend mornings. If you are short on time, try using canned beans.

2 cups dried pinto beans, rinsed and picked clean of stones, or 2 (15-ounce) cans, drained and rinsed

3 tablespoons olive oil

1 yellow onion, diced

2 cloves garlic, minced

2 bay leaves

4 ounces Mushroom and Herb Roast (page 24) or Field Roast Wild Mushroom Quarter Loaf, chopped into ¼-inch pieces

2 teaspoons ground cumin

1 jalapeño pepper, minced

1 tablespoon sea salt

½ teaspoon liquid smoke

1 (14.5-ounce) can diced tomatoes

6 cups water

4 ounces Oaxacan Chili-Spiced Sausage (page 42) or 1 link Field Roast Mexican Chipotle Sausage, crumbled

1. If using dried beans, place in a large bowl and cover with ample water. Allow to soak overnight, or for at least 6 hours.

2. In a stockpot over medium-high heat, heat the olive oil and add the onion, garlic, bay leaves, roast or loaf, cumin, jalapeño, and salt. Stirring occasionally, allow this to cook for 15 minutes, until the onion becomes translucent.

3. Drain the beans from the liquid they were soaked in, and rinse. Add the beans to the stockpot, along with the liquid smoke, tomatoes, and water. Lower the heat to medium-low and cover. Allow to cook for 1½ hours, stirring occasionally.

4. Add the crumbled sausage, and stir to combine. Allow the beans to cook for another 20 minutes, stirring occasionally. Season with salt and serve.

PICKLED MUSTARD GREENS WITH CRISPY NOODLE CAKE

MUSTARD GREENS OFTEN LIVE next to the kale and other leafy vegetables at the grocery store; they're significantly cheaper yet not nearly as popular largely because of their characteristic peppery, pungent flavor. Once pickled, however, the greens aren't nearly as spicy and make for a great addition to a noodle bowl, seasonal stir-fry or even a fresh salad. Here, they're joined with spicy sausage and nian gao: a dried noodle cake that's sliced, soaked, and then fried. These are a rather specific ingredient, but I think you will enjoy working them into your repertoire. You can find nian gao in any Asian grocer. Save some time by making the pickled greens, and soaking the rice cake noodles the day before—that way this can be a quick weeknight dinner affair.

---

1 quart water, for pickling liquid

¼ cup salt

1 quart ice

1 bunch mustard greens, stemmed and roughly chopped

24 ounces rice cake noodles (nian gao)

2 tablespoons safflower oil

¾ pound Oaxacan Chili-Spiced Sausage (page 42) or Field Roast Mexican Chipotle Sausage

2 green onions, sliced

EQUIPMENT

2 (1-quart) mason jars with lids

---

1. Bring 1 quart of water to a boil, add the salt, and then remove from the heat while stirring. When the salt has dissolved, add the quart of ice to cool down the pickling liquid.

2. Distribute the greens and the pickling liquid equally between the two mason jars and allow to rest on the counter overnight. Store in the fridge for up to 1 week.

3. Remove the noodles from the package and cover with room-temperature water. Soak for 2 hours until softened, then drain.

4. In a wok or skillet over medium heat, heat the oil and add the sausage. Sauté until the sausage begins to crisp, about 7 minutes, then add the drained noodles and stir to combine. When the noodles begin to brown around the edges, another 5 to 7 minutes, remove the pan from the heat.

5. Drain the mustard greens and add to the pan to heat through.

6. Garnish with green onion.

CHEF'S NOTE: *American mustard greens are curlier and more closely resemble kale, whereas Chinese mustard greens are darker and flatter like chard leaves. Both types will work here.*

HUNGARIAN CABBAGE SLAW

 **MAKES 5 SERVINGS**

IF YOU'RE A SAUERKRAUT FAN, you're going to love this flavor-packed slaw. And if you're any-thing like me, you'll start finding all kinds of interesting uses for it: spoon it atop your sub sandwich, have it as a side dish with rice pilaf and sausage, or eat a few spoonfuls straight out of the bowl as an afternoon snack. My family roots are German and Irish and both culinary traditions love a good cabbage dish, but so often they're boiled or steamed and, frankly, lifeless. I knew it could be done differently, so here we roast the cabbage to draw out its complex flavor and toss it in a zippy blend of cider vinegar, horseradish, and caraway. Bursting with Eastern European flavors, this recipe is a favorite in our house the second the autumn leaves start turning color, but it's really a simple and inexpensive side dish to make all year round.

1 head green cabbage, thinly sliced

2 teaspoons sea salt

2 red bell peppers, seeded and cut into strips

½ cup cider vinegar

⅓ cup olive oil

3 ounces prepared horseradish

2 tablespoons caraway seeds

3 cloves garlic, minced

1. Toss the cabbage with the salt and let sit for 30 minutes, covered, before draining off any excess liquid.

2. Preheat the oven to 425°F.

3. Combine all the ingredients and arrange, no more than ½ inch deep, on a sheet pan.

4. Roast in the oven for 25 minutes, stirring about halfway through. The cabbage is done once it has begun to caramelize on the edges and most of the liquid has been reduced.

CITRUS AND CHILI SLAW

A MORE ADVENTUROUS TAKE ON your typical coleslaw, this crunchy and refreshing side dish was originally inspired by trips to a tiny town just north of Baja in Mexico. The best part about the town is there's very little to actually do, so we fill the days with beach naps, strolls around town, and cooking simple lunches. Down the road from where we stay is a no-frills town grocery called Oscaritos where we stock up on all the necessities: Pacifico beer, fresh produce, and Popsicles. Although the selection varies widely depending on the day, the shop always seems to have sweet citrus and crisp jicama, an invitation to leisurely walk back to our place and start prepping for an easy lunch slaw. This recipe is great hot weather food and goes really well with Smoky Kalua Jackfruit (page 185), atop your favorite sandwich, or eaten all on its own.

1 orange or minneola, cut into supremes, plus 2 tablespoons of the juice left from cutting the supremes (see Chef's Note, page 108)

2 teaspoons chili powder

⅓ cup cider vinegar

¼ cup olive oil

1 tablespoon freshly squeezed lime juice

2 teaspoons stone-ground mustard

2 cloves garlic

2 teaspoons sea salt

1 tablespoon light brown sugar

½ medium-size head green cabbage, halved, unsightly outer leaves removed, cored, and thinly shredded

1 small to medium-size head radicchio, halved, unsightly outer leaves removed, cored, and thinly shredded

1 small jicama, peeled and julienned

4 sprigs green onion, sliced very thin on a bias

5 sprigs cilantro, large stem pieces removed, roughly chopped

1 serrano pepper, sliced very thinly on the bias

1. In a medium-size bowl, combine the orange juice, chili powder, cider vinegar, oil, lime juice, mustard, garlic, salt, and brown sugar. Whisk well.

2. In a large salad bowl, toss together the cabbage, radicchio, jicama, green onions, cilantro, and serrano.

3. Pour the dressing over the vegetables and toss to coat. Allow to sit for 1 hour before serving.

CARAMEL APPLE BRUSSELS

Delicious!

MAKES 6 SERVINGS

Have a brussels sprouts hater in your life? I'm willing to bet that will all change with this recipe. Brussels sprouts have long been a much maligned vegetable, and I think a lot of that has to do with the way many people prepare them at home: who can really blame kids for hating them boiled or steamed? Thankfully, this recipe takes a serious departure from soggy and flavorless thanks to a quick, sweet glaze featuring the flavors of a caramel apple. The sprouts are then roasted at high heat until they caramelize and become sweet and slightly crisp around the edges. Seriously addicting, and a dish I crave all year round.

1½ pounds Brussels sprouts, sliced in half and soaked in cold water for 10 minutes

¼ cup safflower oil— *did not use*

2 teaspoons sea salt

½ cup cider vinegar

½ cup dark brown sugar

2 teaspoons cornstarch

1 apple, peeled, cored, and ½-inch diced

Leaves from 3 sprigs tarragon, minced

1. Preheat the oven to 475°F.

2. In a large bowl, combine the Brussels sprouts, oil, and sea salt. Toss well. Arrange the Brussels sprouts on a baking sheet and roast in the oven for 7 to 10 minutes, or until the sprouts have a nice caramelization but are still firm. Transfer from the baking sheet to a large mixing bowl and set aside.

3. In a small saucepan over medium heat, combine the cider vinegar and brown sugar and bring to just below a boil. Hold at this heat, stirring occasionally, for 6 minutes, then add the cornstarch and whisk for 2 minutes while the cornstarch dissolves into the mixture. After 2 minutes, lower the heat to a low simmer.

4. Add the apple chunks to the Brussels sprouts, and pour the glaze over the top. Toss to combine, and serve. Garnish with the tarragon.

CHEF'S NOTE: *I like Honeycrisp apples for this recipe because they're sweet and rarely mushy, but you could also use a nice, crisp Granny Smith apple.*

oiled cookie sheet — & parchment.
over $50 — used convection.
8–10 min. Watch! Burn easily.

MISO-GLAZED SQUASH COLLAR

 **MAKES 6 SERVINGS**

INSPIRED BY A JAPANESE CULINARY practice that uses the collar of the fish to avoid waste, this recipe features thick slices of red kuri squash brushed with miso, citrus, and soy and slow roasted until soft and fragrant. While you could certainly use any squash you like here, the flesh of the red kuri is a beautiful vibrant orange, superrich in flavor and creamy in texture—and it never gets mushy or stringy. I love this recipe warm, right out of the oven, with a cold glass of beer. Straddling the line between sweet and savory, it makes a great, healthy snack or a satisfying vegetarian side dish.

1 red kuri squash

3 tablespoons safflower oil

1 teaspoon sea salt

1 orange, zested and juiced

3 tablespoons white or yellow miso paste

3 tablespoons soy sauce or liquid aminos

1. Preheat the oven to 425°F.

2. Slice the top off the squash and clean out the seeds and membrane with a sturdy spoon.

3. Slice the squash vertically into ¾-inch "ribs."

4. Toss the squash slices in the oil and salt. Place on a sheet pan and roast in the oven for 25 minutes.

5. In a saucepan over medium-low heat, combine the orange zest and juice, miso, and soy sauce. Allow to reduce by half to make a syrupy glaze.

6. Brush the glaze over the squash and return it to the oven for 8 minutes, or until the glaze caramelizes.

COCONUT RICE

I HAVE TO GIVE A SHOUT-OUT HERE to my favorite heavy metal–loving vegan chef in the business, Chris Gaye. I had the pleasure of working with Chris at PCC, a beloved Seattle-area grocery co-op, and while coconut rice isn't necessarily a new or novel concept, it was his idea to add wild rice to our recipe. A great substitute for sticky rice and a simple recipe to tackle at home when you're ready to take your rice game to the next level, the mild coconut flavor complements hot or spicy dishes beautifully, and the wild rice adds a pleasant nutty flavor and chewy texture. Simple enough to make on a busy weeknight, but interesting enough to make for your next dinner party or gathering with friends.

¼ cup wild rice

2½ cups water

2 cups medium-grain white rice

½ (13.5-ounce) can full-fat coconut milk

1. In a saucepan over medium heat, combine the wild rice and ½ cup of the water. Simmer until the rice begins to open up, about 15 minutes. Remove from the heat, drain off any excess water, and set aside.

2. Rinse the white rice in a medium-size saucepan, then drain.

3. Add the wild rice, coconut milk, and remaining 2 cups of water to the pan and stir. Bring to a boil over medium-high heat. Stir once, lower heat to a low simmer, and cover.

4. Cook for 20 minutes. Turn off the burner and allow the rice to sit, covered, for an additional 20 minutes.

5. Remove the lid, fluff the rice, and serve.

RANCH POTATOES

MY GRANDMA LIVES ON A breezy farm on the Olympic Peninsula, a lush bit of land a few hours west of Seattle. Although bulk spices and grains are popular (even trendy!) today, they certainly weren't that way decades ago, but my grandma was ahead of her time: her spice drawer is enviable and is always stocked to the brim with bulk herbs, spices, and her own signature blends. These potatoes are a very simple, oven-roasted preparation but are made special, thanks to my grandma's homemade ranch spice blend. I've asked many times what's in them and she'll never tell, so I made some guesses here and have gotten pretty darn close. For days when the drive to the farm seems a bit too far, these are the next best thing.

3 pounds Yukon Gold potatoes

2 tablespoons safflower oil

2 teaspoons sea salt

2 teaspoons curry powder

1 teaspoon ground cumin

1 teaspoon smoked paprika

1 teaspoon dried marjoram

1 teaspoon dried coriander

1 teaspoon freshly ground black pepper

1 teaspoon celery salt

1. Preheat the oven to 375°F.

2. Wash and scrub the potatoes thoroughly.

3. Wedge cut the potatoes about the size of an orange slice, and soak in cold water for 5 minutes to remove the starch.

4. Drain and allow the potatoes to dry.

5. Combine the potatoes, oil, salt, herbs, and spices and place on a sheet pan.

6. Roast in the oven for 35 to 40 minutes, turning the potatoes about halfway through.

7. Remove from the pan, and serve immediately.

BERBERE ROASTED ROOTS

 **MAKES 6 SERVINGS**

FOR THE LAST TEN YEARS I've been lucky enough to live in south Seattle, home to many of the city's best Ethiopian restaurants. If you've spent much time sampling this vibrant, flavor-packed cuisine, you've likely encountered berbere spice, a common African blend that varies by region and town but that often features fenugreek, paprika, chiles, garlic, and ginger. Most well-stocked grocery stores will carry a version in the spice section. It's a spice worth celebrating and this recipe does just that, with a fusion of Ethiopian flavors and Pacific Northwest root vegetables. It makes for a simple and comforting side dish during the fall and winter months, and is always a welcome addition to the holiday table.

1 pound potatoes

2 medium-size parsnips

1 large red beet

3 carrots

1 turnip

½ cup coconut oil

3 tablespoons berbere spice

1. Preheat the oven to 350°F.

2. Peel all the root vegetables and cut them into 1-inch chunks.

3. In a small saucepan over low heat, combine the coconut oil and berbere spice. Simmer for 3 to 4 minutes. Remove from the heat. Toss the root chunks with the spice mixture and arrange on a sheet pan.

4. Bake for 35 to 40 minutes, or until tender and starting to brown, stirring halfway through.

CHEF'S NOTE: *Feel free to use whatever combination of root vegetables (about 6 pounds total) that you prefer or that are in season.*

PARSNIP ROOT WHIP

WHEN YOU'RE READY TO DEVIATE from your standard mashed potato recipe, this creamy root whip is by far the best place to start. Parsnips bring a complex sweetness, while the celery root is creamy and slightly herbaceous. When you're shopping for parsnips, try to select smaller ones as they're going to be more tender and easier to work with. And as with any mashed potato recipe, you want to cut the root vegetables into large pieces, as smaller pieces will absorb more water and will prohibit you from getting that airy fluffiness we all love. To bring this dish together, I love Kite Hill brand cream cheese, but vegan sour cream can stand in as a substitute if you can't get your hands on it.

5 teaspoons sea salt

1 pound Yukon Gold potatoes, peeled

⅔ pound celery root, peeled and cut into 1-inch pieces (see Chef's Note, page 126)

⅔ pound parsnips, peeled and cut into 1-inch pieces

6 ounces plain vegan cream cheese

5⅓ tablespoons vegan butter, cut into ½-inch pieces

Pinch of white pepper

Leaves from 2 sprigs thyme, chopped

1. Fill a large pot with water, add 1 tablespoon of the salt, and bring to a boil over high heat.

2. Add the potatoes and allow to cook for 10 minutes before adding the celery root and parsnip.

3. Allow to cook for another 15 to 20 minutes over high heat, or until potatoes are tender when pierced with a knife.

4. Remove from the heat and drain in a colander. Allow the hot vegetables to sit for 3 to 4 minutes while the excess water evaporates.

5. In a large mixing bowl, combine the vegetables and mash with a large whisk or potato masher. Fold in the remaining ingredients, except the thyme. When the vegetables are fully mashed, you may need to fully combine everything with a large spoon or rubber spatula, being careful not to overmix.

6. Serve hot, garnished with the thyme.

CHEF'S NOTE: *To avoid overmixing (and the gumminess that will inevitably follow), mash the root vegetables first before folding in the other ingredients.*

SMOKED OYSTER MUSHROOM STUFFING

 **MAKES 8 SERVINGS**

W HILE I COME ACROSS new cookbooks all the time, the one I probably revisit most frequently is this cool seventies-era book that features interesting regional takes on classic recipes—such as stuffing. Some people love chestnuts in their stuffing and others are adamant that corn bread is the only way to go, but here in the Pacific Northwest we love our oysters. So, this recipe is an homage to our region, but instead of oysters we use oyster mushrooms. They're really tender and meaty and relatively easy to find during the fall and winter months. The sweet apple and smoky sausage round out all the big flavors here, making this one of my favorite parts of the holiday meal.

2 tablespoons olive oil

4 tablespoons vegan butter

1 yellow onion, ¼-inch diced

2 stalks celery, ¼-inch diced

7 ounces Smoked Potato and Artichoke Sausage (page 40) or 2 links Field Roast Smoked Apple Sage Sausage, crumbled

1 apple, cored and ¼-inch diced

½ pound oyster mushrooms, brushed clean and separated at the base, any woody stems removed

1 fennel bulb, halved, cored, and ¼-inch diced

2 cloves garlic, minced

1 tablespoon dried rubbed sage

Leaves from 4 sprigs thyme, chopped

Leaves from 2 sprigs rosemary, chopped

1 tablespoon sea salt

½ cup white wine

1 loaf vegan crusty artisan bread, cut into ¾-inch cubes and allowed to air-dry overnight

1 cup Mushroom and Herb Stock (page 196) or vegan mushroom stock

Safflower or canola oil spray

1. Preheat the oven to 375°F. In a skillet over medium heat, heat the oil and vegan butter and add the onion, celery, sausage, apple, mushrooms, fennel, garlic, sage, thyme, rosemary, and salt. Sauté, stirring occasionally, for 10 to 15 minutes, or until the vegetables are soft. Add the wine and stir, scraping any bits that have begun to stick to the bottom of the pan.

3. Transfer the mixture to a large mixing bowl and add the bread cubes. Toss with a large spoon or your hands to combine. Add the stock and lightly toss again.

4. Transfer the stuffing to a baking dish that has been sprayed with oil. Let the stuffing sit for at least 30 minutes before baking.

5. Bake for 35 minutes, or until crusty on top. Alternatively, you may use this as a stuffing for the filling in a roast, or to stuff vegetables, such as peppers or squash.

CHEF'S NOTE: *You want stale bread for this recipe, and if you're in a hurry to get started and your bread's not yet stale, simply cube it and let it sit out for half a day or so, to get nice and crusty.*

CAULIFLOWER GRATIN

T HIS EASY SIDE DISH IS COMFORT FOOD at its best, and ends up making an appearance on our table throughout the cooler weather months. It's a great accompaniment to the Mushroom and Herb Roast (page 24) and Steakhouse Roast (page 27), and can be adapted to include other root vegetables, such as parsnips, potatoes or even rutabagas—so, mix and swap as you please. If I've got them on hand, I'll dress up this gratin with a handful of fresh, chopped herbs or add a pinch of chili powder and smoked paprika for more of a Southwest vibe. Really, it's hard to go wrong.

---

1 tablespoon plus 1 teaspoon sea salt

8 cups ice

1 head cauliflower, divided into bite-size florets

2 tablespoons olive oil

1 yellow onion, sliced

1 large shallot, sliced

2 sprigs thyme

1 tablespoon Dijon mustard

2 cups Vegan Béchamel (page 192), plus more if desired

Safflower or canola oil spray

⅔ cup bread crumbs

---

1. Fill a large pot with water, add 1 tablespoon of the salt, and bring to a boil over high heat.

2. In a large bowl, combine 8 cups of ice with 8 cups of water.

3. Add the cauliflower to the boiling water, cover, and blanch for 3 minutes.

4. Drain the cauliflower and transfer to the bowl of ice water, stirring once to ensure the cauliflower cools rapidly. When the cauliflower has cooled, drain and set aside.

5. In a skillet over medium-low heat, heat 1 tablespoon of the oil and add the onion, shallot, thyme, and the 1 teaspoon of salt. Cook, stirring occasionally, until the onion and shallot have begun to caramelize, about 25 minutes.

6. Meanwhile, preheat the oven to 400°F.

7. In a large bowl, combine the cauliflower, onion mixture, Dijon, and 1 cup of the béchamel. Toss to fully coat.

8. Transfer the cauliflower to a baking dish or individual ramekins sprayed with oil. Pour the remaining cup of béchamel into the dish or dishes (you can add more if you prefer a creamier gratin).

9. Top the cauliflower with the bread crumbs and drizzle with the remaining tablespoon of oil. Place the baking dish or dishes on a baking sheet, and bake for 25 to 30 minutes, or until the cauliflower is bubbling and golden brown.

MACARONI & CHAO

WHEN WE LAUNCHED OUR Field Roast Chao Cheese, we had our priorities straight. First order of business: make a killer vegan macaroni and cheese that would be comforting, creamy and crave-worthy . . . all without the dairy. This recipe uses my Vegan Béchamel (page 192) for the base as well as our Chao Cheese, but the thing that makes it truly special is the torn, crusty bread on top. Drizzled with olive oil and topped with fresh herbs, the bread topping really raises the bar on what macaroni and cheese can and should be. While it's perfect as is, I love scheming up ways to dress up my mac with such toppings as pickled peppers, sautéed kale, additional fresh herbs, or sliced sausage.

1 pound elbow macaroni noodles

4 cups Vegan Béchamel (page 192)

1 package Field Roast Creamy Original Chao Cheese Slices, sliced or shredded into small pieces

Safflower or canola oil spray

¼ loaf vegan crusty sourdough bread, torn into small pieces

2 tablespoons olive oil

Leaves from 3 sprigs oregano, roughly chopped

Leaves from 3 sprigs dill, roughly chopped

Leaves from 3 sprigs thyme, roughly chopped

2 pickled peppers, sliced (I like Mama Lil's)

1. Preheat the oven to 350°F.

2. Boil the pasta in salted water until al dente; drain, but do not rinse.

3. Combine the cooked pasta with the béchamel and Chao Cheese and transfer to a baking dish that has been sprayed with oil.

4. Top the pasta with the bread pieces and drizzle with the olive oil.

5. Bake for 35 minutes, or until the bread topping begins to crisp.

6. Remove from the oven and garnish with the herbs and pickled peppers.

FRANK FRIED RICE

M Y VEGAN VERSION OF HAWAIIAN Spam fried rice relies on Field Roast Frankfurters, kimchi for a punch of flavor, and peas for a nostalgic pop of color. I love this stuff. When you fry the rice, it's good to work in small batches so you get those craveable crispy bits, and that just won't happen if the rice is all jumbled on top of itself. Here I call for already cooked rice, so this is a great one to pull out when you've got leftover rice in the fridge and little inspiration at the ready. It's always a popular potluck or picnic recipe, but if you want me to be honest: it's got breakfast written all over it, which is why I often make a double batch to ensure I have leftovers the next day. If you don't have Field Roast Frankfurters on hand, feel free to use your favorite grain meat in their place.

2 tablespoons safflower oil

1 tablespoon minced fresh ginger

3 green onions, sliced

1 carrot, peeled and ¼-inch diced

2 Field Roast Frankfurters, ¼-inch diced

2 cloves garlic

¼ cup kimchi, finely chopped, juices reserved

½ teaspoon freshly ground black pepper

3 cups cooked short- or medium-grain white rice

2 teaspoons sesame oil

2 tablespoons mirin

2 tablespoons tamari or cultured shoyu

½ cup frozen peas

4 sprigs cilantro, large stems removed, chopped

1. In a wok over high heat, heat the safflower oil and add the ginger, green onions, and carrot. Cook, stirring every 10 seconds, for 2 minutes, then add the diced frankfurters, garlic, kimchi and its juices, and pepper.

2. Let this mixture cook, stirring every 10 to 15 seconds, for another 3 minutes, then add the rice, sesame oil, mirin, and tamari and stir to combine. Continue to cook, stirring this every 15 to 20 seconds, for 2 minutes; the rice will start getting crispy in spots.

3. Add the peas, stir, and remove from the heat.

4. Plate the rice and garnish with cilantro leaves.

APPETIZERS

HOM BAO

I F YOU'RE NOT FAMILIAR WITH hom bao, it's a steamed bun that you often get if you're going out to dim sum or to a Chinese restaurant. Here in Seattle at Pike Place Market, a small Chinese pastry shop, wedged between a bunch of produce stands, makes what I think is the very best bao. As a kid my favorite was always the Corn and Mayonnaise Bao, which no one else in my family liked. Which was just fine by me. This recipe is a shout-out to that beloved snack, but it's also a different take on hom bao, which is usually made with sweet BBQ sauce. Here, I use our roast instead and steam the buns to remain true to the original. They're just as good as—if not better than—how I remember them back in the day.

1⅓ cups warm water (100°F)

1 tablespoon sugar

1⅔ teaspoons instant yeast

4 cups all-purpose flour

3 tablespoons safflower oil

2½ teaspoons baking powder

1 teaspoon sea salt

FILLING

1 tablespoon olive oil

1 medium-size shallot, minced

8 ounces Lemongrass and Ginger Roast (page 18) or Field Roast Lentil Sage Quarter Loaf, ¼-inch diced

1 cup frozen corn kernels

2 teaspoons sea salt

2 tablespoons seasoned rice wine vinegar

½ cup vegan mayo

3 sprigs dill, large stems removed, minced

EQUIPMENT

Steamer basket

1. In a mixing bowl, combine the warm water, sugar, yeast, and ¼ cup of the flour. Whisk together and let sit for 15 minutes as the yeast activates.

2. Add the remaining 3¾ cups of flour and the oil, baking powder, and salt. Bring the ingredients together by stirring with a spoon. Once fully combined, transfer the dough to a board and begin kneading. Knead for 6 to 7 minutes, or until the dough no longer sticks to your hands. If the dough is sticking, add a sprinkle of flour and continue kneading. Transfer the dough back to the bowl and allow to rise for 1 hour, or until it has doubled in size.

3. Prepare the filling: In a skillet over medium heat, heat the oil, shallot, roast or loaf, and corn. Sauté, stirring occasionally, for 10 minutes. Add the salt and vinegar, stir, and remove from the heat. Transfer the mixture to a bowl and add the mayo and dill. Stir to combine.

4. Lightly punch down the dough after it has risen. Divide the dough into twelve pieces and roll each into a ball. Roll out each ball into a 4-inch flat circle. Spoon a decent scoop of the filling onto the center, then bring the sides up around the filling and twist the dough shut at the top. Let the buns rest for 30 minutes.

5. Place the bao in a steamer and steam for 15 minutes.

CHEF'S NOTES: *When you steam the bao, just be sure not to lift the lid: they have double the leavening (yeast and baking powder) so you get a lot of rise, but if you open the lid too soon, they'll fall.*

PANZANELLA SKEWERS

 **MAKES 6 SERVINGS**

I LOVE BREAD SALADS and I really love grilled bread salads, but the problem is that so often the bread becomes soggy. I set out to fix that, creating this deconstructed bread salad on a skewer to take advantage of all of the fresh flavors of a panzanella salad without the sogginess. These make a great party appetizer, and are simple enough to take to a barbecue and grill on-site. If you're going to use fresh bread, it's a good idea to cut it into thick slices and let it sit out for a day or so to dry out, making it sturdy enough to grill. And if you have leftover herbed oil, it's wonderful drizzled on top of seasonal soups and salads.

⅓ cup balsamic vinegar

1 sprig rosemary

Leaves from 2 sprigs dill

Leaves from 3 sprigs oregano

¼ ounce fresh basil (about 12 leaves)

1 clove garlic

⅓ cup olive oil, plus more for grilling

8 ounces cherry tomatoes

3 links Fennel and Garlic Sausage (page 38) or Field Roast Italian Sausage, sliced on the bias into ¾-inch-thick pieces

8 ounces vegan crusty artisan bread, torn or cut into ¾- to 1-inch cubes

EQUIPMENT

20 medium-length wooden or bamboo skewers, soaked in cold water for 2 hours

1. Place the balsamic vinegar and rosemary sprig in a saucepan over low to medium heat. Allow this to reduce to about ¼ cup in volume, then remove from the heat and strain. Monitor carefully as it will start to evaporate quickly. Set aside.

2. In a blender, combine the dill, oregano, basil, garlic, and olive oil. Process until smooth and green and set aside.

3. Preheat a grill or grill pan over medium heat.

4. Assemble the presoaked skewers with tomato, sausage, and then bread to finish.

5. Before grilling, drizzle a small amount of olive oil over the skewers.

6. Grill the skewers on two sides until slightly charred. Remove and plate to serve immediately.

7. Drizzle a small amount of herbed oil on plate or platter, top with skewers, then finish with a drizzle of a bit more herbed oil and reduced balsamic vinegar.

SPICY CORN AND CHILI FRITTERS

I WAS ONCE ASKED TO MAKE a simple southern appetizer for a co-worker's wife's birthday celebration, and after a lot of tweaking, these addictive fritters are eventually where I landed—for a few reasons. First, they're really simple and take only ten minutes to make. Second, when fresh corn is at the height of its season, there's nothing better than that natural sweetness it brings. Serve these with Avocado Ranch Dressing (page 198), and if fresh corn isn't in season, just swap in thawed frozen corn instead.

3 cups safflower or another high-heat oil, such as canola, peanut, or vegetable, for frying

½ cup unsweetened plain almond milk, cold

2 tablespoons Follow Your Heart vegan egg

½ cup all-purpose flour

1 teaspoon baking powder

1 teaspoon chili powder

1 teaspoon sugar

1 teaspoon sea salt

4 ounces Oaxacan Chili-Spiced Sausage (page 42) or 1 link Field Roast Mexican Chipotle Sausage, crumbled

8 sprigs chives, minced

1 (5-ounce) can green chiles, drained

1 cup corn kernels, lightly roasted in the oven or sliced off an already cooked cob

Avocado Ranch Dressing, for serving (page 198)

1. In a heavy-bottomed pot, heat the oil to 375°F.

2. In a blender, combine the milk and vegan egg and blend for 2 minutes. Set aside.

3. In a large mixing bowl, combine the flour, baking powder, chili powder, sugar, and salt. Whisk well. Add the remaining ingredients, including milk mixture, and mix until combined.

4. Spoon a little less than ¼ cup of the batter into the oil at a time. Fry for 4 to 5 minutes, or until the fritters are golden brown. Transfer to a paper towel–lined plate. Serve with Avocado Ranch Dressing.

WHITE BEAN AND EGGPLANT CROSTINI

A GREAT MAKE-AHEAD APPETIZER and always the first to go at any picnic or barbecue, this summery crostini begins with a simple white bean and eggplant mixture, but is quickly taken up a notch with the addition of two unlikely ingredients: oil-cured olives and nectarines. This recipe is all about contrasts in flavor: the creamy white beans jut up against the sweet stone fruit and salty olives, making for an intriguing and most memorable bite. When I'm organized enough to plan out my week, I'll double the white bean topping and use it on salads and sandwiches or as a hearty snack when I get home from work and need something to tide me over until dinner.

1 vegan baguette, cut on the bias into ¼-inch-thick slices

⅓ cup olive oil

1 medium-size or 2 small Asian eggplants, peeled and cut into ¼-inch pieces

2 teaspoons sea salt, plus more for seasoning

4 cloves garlic, minced

6 dry-cured olives, pitted and minced

1 (15-ounce) can cannellini beans, drained and rinsed

⅓ cup balsamic vinegar

1 nectarine, pitted and chopped

Leaves from 4 sprigs oregano, roughly chopped

¼ cup vegan mayo (optional)

2 ounces microgreens

Leaves from ¼ bunch parsley, minced

1. Preheat the oven to 350°F.

2. Place the baguette slices on a sheet pan and drizzle with 1 tablespoon of the oil.

3. Toast in the oven for 7 to 10 minutes, or until the slices are crispy throughout.

4. In a skillet over medium heat, place the eggplant first, stir, and then add the salt and all but 1 tablespoon of the remaining oil. Cook, stirring occasionally, adding the garlic and olives after 3 to 4 minutes.

5. Allow the mixture to cook over medium heat for an additional 15 minutes, stirring occasionally. Once the eggplant becomes soft, add the beans, vinegar, nectarine, and oregano.

6. Stir the mixture, allowing it to come back up to temperature. Once the vinegar begins to coat the beans, remove from the heat and set aside.

7. Toss the greens with the reserved tablespoon of oil.

8. Top each toasted baguette slice with a smear of mayo, if desired, a scoop of the eggplant mixture, and then a pinch of microgreens. Garnish with parsley.

GRILLED FRESH ROLLS, PAGE 156

GRILLED FRESH ROLLS

A FEW YEARS AGO, FIELD ROAST was located on Jackson Street in the International District of Seattle, a vibrant bustling neighborhood often known as Little Saigon. Our office was steps away from a handful of Vietnamese restaurants, and that's where you could often find me during the lunch hour. Fresh rolls are a popular appetizer in Vietnamese restaurants and traditionally they're made with minced raw vegetables or cold noodles, resulting in a superfresh, light snack. After sampling more fresh rolls than I care to admit, I was inspired to hop into the ring and create a slightly more substantial version with bits of our grilled sausage in the mix. The result is a flavorful, hearty roll that can double as lunch any day of the week. These rolls are best served within a few hours of preparing, ideally with your favorite sweet chili or peanut sauce.

4 ounces thin rice noodles

2 links Fennel and Garlic Sausage (page 38) or Field Roast Italian Sausage, sliced lengthwise

1 teaspoon safflower oil

8 spring roll wrappers

8 lettuce leaves

Leaves from 4 sprigs mint

Leaves from 10 leaves basil, cut into chiffonade

Leaves from 5 sprigs cilantro

2 green onions, green tops sliced very thinly on the bias so they curl

¼ pound small daikon radish, peeled and cut into matchsticks

2 medium-size carrots, peeled and cut into matchsticks

1 medium-size cucumber, peeled, seeded, and cut into ¼-inch pieces

1 jalapeño pepper, cut into thin strips (optional)

Sweet chili sauce, for dipping

1. Place the rice noodles in a large bowl and cover with hot (just shy of boiling) water. Allow to soak for 5 minutes, or until soft. Drain off the excess water and set aside.

2. In a skillet or on a grill over medium heat, brush the sausage with oil and grill for 3 minutes on each side. Remove from the heat, and slice each half into two shorter pieces.

3. Build the rolls one at a time: Place a spring roll wrapper in a bowl of warm water just long enough to thoroughly wet the wrapper. Remove the wrapper and allow any excess moisture to drip off.

4. Set the wrapper on a clean work surface and begin stacking ingredients: lettuce leaf, noodles, sausage, herbs, daikon, carrot, cucumber, and jalapeño, if using. Do not try to overload the roll or else the wrapper will rip.

5. Roll up the wrapper like a burrito, tucking in the filling on both sides.

6. The rolls should be served within a few hours, with sweet chili sauce on the side for dipping.

CHEF'S NOTE: *The fresh roll wrappers can be a bit tricky to work with if you haven't done so before. The key is to set up a nice, clean board with lots of space to work. Also, make sure your water is about the temperature that you would use to wash your hands: hot but not scalding. Take your time when you get to the rolling process. Begin by pulling up the side that is closest to you first, then fold in the sides on the left and the right, and finish by rolling it over the final edge away from your body. This is a process that will take a good two or three tries to get right. Don't worry if a few don't look perfect, you'll be a pro soon enough!*

PICADILLO EMPANADAS

THESE HANDHELD MEAT PASTRIES have a lot going for them, but before I sing their praises, this is most definitely a recipe I'd love for you to adapt and make your own. Picadillo is a regional dish in many Latin American countries, made with ground meat, tomatoes, sometimes olives or capers, occasionally raisins or peppers—it depends on where you live and who's cooking. It's often served with rice or used as a filling for tacos or savory empanadas, which is what I especially love. If there's an ingredient you don't care for here, leave it out. If you are looking to use up some dried fruits or nuts, toss them in. Extra olives? Great. The crust recipe is one of my favorites, too, as it can be sweet or savory, so you can always make a double batch and freeze half for later.

PASTRY

2½ cups all-purpose flour, plus more for dusting

1 teaspoon salt

12 tablespoons (1½ sticks) vegan butter, sliced and thoroughly chilled

¼ cup unsweetened plain almond milk, very cold

FILLING

3 tablespoons safflower oil

1 pound Fennel and Garlic Sausage (page 38) or Field Roast Italian Sausage, crumbled

1 yellow onion, ¼-inch diced

4 cloves garlic, minced

1 tablespoon chili powder

2 bay leaves

1 tablespoon sea salt

1 very ripe tomato, ¼-inch diced

⅔ cup green olives, chopped

1 tablespoon tomato paste

2 tablespoons cider vinegar

¼ cup raisins

OPTIONAL GLAZE

¼ cup safflower oil

2 teaspoons cornstarch

1. First, prepare the pastry: In a food processor, combine the flour and salt and blend together. Add the chunks of vegan butter and pulse until they become the size of small peas. Add the milk and pulse a few times until the dough starts to come together, but is still loose. Turn out the contents of the food processor onto a floured board. Bring the dough together by lightly working it with your hand.

2. The crust will still be a little crumbly, but divide into two equal parts and transfer to a resealable bag or plastic wrap. Wrap each piece together tightly in a disk shape and transfer to the fridge to chill for 1½ hours.

3. Prepare the filling: In a skillet over medium heat, heat 2 tablespoons of the oil and add the crumbled sausage. Lightly brown the sausage, stirring occasionally, 5 to 6 minutes. Remove the sausage from the pan and set aside. Return the pan to medium heat and add the onion, garlic, chili powder, bay leaves, remaining tablespoon of oil, and the salt. Cook this mixture, stirring occasionally, for about 10 minutes, or until the onion is translucent.

4. Add the remaining ingredients, including the sausage, lower the heat to medium-low, and simmer for 20 minutes, stirring occasionally. Taste the mixture and adjust for salt. Remove from the heat and cool the mixture in the fridge for 2 hours.

5. Remove the dough from the fridge and let sit on the counter for 10 minutes. Divide the dough into 2-inch pieces and roll into balls.

6. On a floured surface, roll out the balls into flat circles. Fill half of each circle with a little less than ¼ cup of filling. Fold the clean half over the filling and crimp the dough where it meets the other side, using a fork.

7. Chill the stuffed empanadas in the fridge for at least 30 minutes.

8. Meanwhile, preheat the oven to 425°F.

9. Place the empanadas on a parchment paper–lined sheet pan and bake for 25 to 30 minutes, or until golden brown. For a nice sheen, combine ¼ cup oil with 2 teaspoons of cornstarch in a blender. Brush this on the empanadas about halfway through the baking process.

CHEF'S NOTE: *While we don't use a traditional egg wash in our baking, you can still get that nice golden sheen on the top of your pastry by brushing on a mixture of oil and cornstarch about halfway through the baking process.*

CHIOGGIA BEET TARTARE WITH VEGAN EGG YOLK

 **MAKES 5 SERVINGS**

THIS RECIPE COMES FROM a vegan dinner collaboration that Field Roast did at Orfeo restaurant in Seattle with chef Kevin Davis. Our "hit it out of the park" dish was this beautiful beet tartare that we all ended up talking about (and craving!) for weeks to follow. We assembled the tartare by layering the Chioggia beets in a ring mold, but if you don't have one at home, simply slice off the top and bottom of an aluminum can and use it exactly the same way: your tartare will be just as pretty.

½ vegan baguette, sliced ¼-inch thick and brushed with olive oil

1 tablespoon sea salt, plus more for garnish

2 medium-size Chioggia beets, cleaned

¼ cup water

1½ teaspoons Follow Your Heart vegan egg

2 tablespoons freshly squeezed lemon juice

2 teaspoons Dijon mustard

1 teaspoon vegan Worcestershire sauce

2 teaspoons Champagne vinegar

2 tablespoons olive oil, plus more for serving

1 small shallot, minced

1 sprig parsley, large stems removed, minced

2 cornichons, minced, plus more for serving, if desired

Leaves from 1 sprig oregano

2 tablespoons capers

Freshly ground black pepper

OPTIONAL GARNISH

1 tablespoon Vegg vegan egg

¼ cup cold water

EQUIPMENT

5 (3-inch) ring molds (see headnote)

1. Preheat the oven to 350°F. Arrange the baguette slices on a baking sheet. Bake for 8 to 10 minutes, or until the slices are crispy. Remove from the pan and set aside.

2. In medium-size pot over high heat, bring 6 cups of water and the salt to a boil. Add the beets and cook for 30 minutes. Drain the beets and allow to cool for at least 15 minutes before peeling. Peel and transfer the beets to the fridge to fully cool, about 2 hours.

3. In a blender, blend together the ¼ cup of water and vegan egg, lemon juice, Dijon, Worcestershire, and Champagne vinegar. While blending, slowly drizzle in the olive oil, allowing the mixture to emulsify. When the oil is fully combined, stop the blender and set the mixture aside.

4. Remove the beets from the fridge and mince roughly. In a large mixing bowl, combine the beets, blended dressing, shallots, parsley, cornichons, oregano, and capers. Fold the mixture together gently. Spoon the beet mixture into a 3-inch ring mold and press down to form a puck shape that is about 1-inch thick. Repeat for additional servings.

5. Serve with additional cornichons, if using, and toasted baguette slices. Garnish with black pepper and sea salt and a drizzle of good olive oil. You can also garnish with a small amount of the Vegg blended with cold water, to serve as a vegan egg yolk.

SAUSAGE-STUFFED TOMATOES WITH TOMATO JUS

MAKES 6 SERVINGS

MANY PEOPLE WHO HAVE NEVER visited Seattle envision it as a rain-cloaked, gray city for much of the year. The truth is: summer (and fall) days are often sunny and hot enough to grow some real-deal tomatoes. Come August, we end up having a real glut of them, which I realize sounds like an enviable problem, but I hate food waste. I always have to get a bit creative in using them up before any go bad besides making tomato sauce and slicing them up for salads. You want to choose a good-size, relatively firm tomato because you're going to scrape the insides and strain them to make tomato gravy—a simple process that makes the whole house smell like a late summer farmhouse.

6 medium-size to large on-the-vine tomatoes

3 tablespoons olive oil

1 yellow onion, ¼-inch diced

1 zucchini, ¼-inch diced

1 green bell pepper, ¼-inch diced

1 teaspoon freshly ground black pepper

2 teaspoons sea salt

2 links Fennel and Garlic Sausage (page 38) or Field Roast Italian Sausage, crumbled

¾ cup vegan bread crumbs

1 tablespoon tomato paste

2 sprigs oregano

1 teaspoon sugar

2 cloves garlic, minced

1. Preheat the oven to 400°F. Slice the top off each tomato. Using a spoon, scoop out the insides, membrane, and seeds, using a paring knife to separate the membrane from the rest of the tomato. Set the tomato shells aside. Place the insides in a fine-mesh sieve or screen over a bowl. Squeeze the contents through the sieve into the bowl and set aside, discarding any remaining solids.

2. In a skillet over medium heat, heat 2 tablespoons of the oil and add the onion, zucchini, bell pepper, black pepper, and salt. Sauté, stirring occasionally, for 5 minutes. Add the sausage and continue to cook for another 5 to 7 minutes, until the sausage is heated throughout. Remove from the heat. Add ½ cup of the bread crumbs and stir to combine. Using a spoon, equally divide the filling among the tomatoes until they are full, while gently pressing the filling to ensure each tomato is adequately stuffed.

3. In a small saucepan over medium heat, whisk together the juices from the tomatoes with the tomato paste, oregano, sugar, and garlic. Stirring occasionally, allow the mixture to reduce by a quarter. Remove from the heat and strain.

4. Arrange the tomatoes in a baking dish, top them with the remaining ¼ cup of bread crumbs, and drizzle with the remaining tablespoon of oil. Bake for 20 minutes.

5. Remove the tomatoes from the dish, and serve, ladling a small amount of the tomato juice mixture over each one.

SPICED SAUSAGE AND LEEK FLATBREAD

H OMEMADE FLATBREAD IS A CINCH when you have the dough on hand, and for this flavorful recipe I use my Slow Poke Pizza Dough (page 200) along with my very favorite olives: vibrant, creamy Castelvetranos. Then, I layer on sweet leeks and a good bit of garlic, fresh herbs, and smoky sausage. The result is, honestly, the flatbread recipe that I crave the most and the one our friends continue to request when they come to visit. In lieu of cheese, I boil the garlic to make a creamy base sauce. And, bonus: no need for a pizza stone or fancy equipment: you can just roll this dough out and bake it in your home oven.

3 teaspoons sea salt

10 cloves garlic, peeled and left whole

Leaves from 2 sprigs oregano

1 teaspoon freshly ground black pepper

¼ cup plus 2 tablespoons olive oil, plus more for brushing

3 medium-size leeks, washed (see Chef's Note) and cut into ½-inch slices up to the tops, tough green ends discarded

3 sprigs thyme

3 tablespoons white wine

1 lemon, cut into ⅛-inch slices

2 links Oaxacan Chili-Spiced Sausage (page 42) or Field Roast Mexican Chipotle Sausage, sliced ¼ inch thick

½ cup Castelvetrano olives, pitted and sliced

2 teaspoons red pepper flakes

1 tablespoon cornmeal

All-purpose flour, for dusting

1 pound Slow Poke Pizza Dough (page 200) or your favorite vegan pizza dough, removed from fridge about 1 hour before you plan to grill

1. Preheat the oven to 450 °F.

2. In a small saucepan, bring 2 cups water and 1 teaspoon of the salt to a boil, add the garlic cloves, and cook for 10 minutes. Drain the garlic and transfer to a food processor or blender (discarding the cooking water). Add the oregano, 1 teaspoon of the salt, the black pepper, and ¼ cup of the olive oil to the garlic and process until smooth.

3. In a skillet over medium-low heat, heat the remaining 2 tablespoons of oil and add the leeks, thyme, and the remaining teaspoon of salt. After 5 minutes, lower the heat to low and allow the leeks to cook, stirring occasionally, until they begin to caramelize, 20 to 25 minutes. Deglaze the pan with the wine, stirring to combine, and let reduce until the liquid is gone from the bottom of the pan, 2 to 3 minutes. Transfer the leek mixture to a bowl and set aside, discarding the thyme sprigs.

4. Brush the lemon slices with a little oil and grill over high heat for 3 minutes per side, or until they have some visible grill marks. If you do not have a grill available, you can use a skillet heated over medium-high heat for 3 minutes per side.

5. Brush a 12 x 17-inch baking sheet with oil and sprinkle with cornmeal. Sprinkle a clean surface with a little flour and roll out the pizza dough, shaping it to fit the baking sheet. Spread the garlic mixture evenly across the dough, using a rubber spatula or brush, making sure to coat the dough all the way to the edge. Layer the dough with the leek mixture, sausage, and olives.

6. Transfer the pan to the oven and bake for 15 to18 minutes, or until the crust begins to brown. Remove the flatbread from the pan and garnish with grilled lemon slices and red pepper flakes.

CHEF'S NOTE: *Leeks can be pretty dirty. To wash them thoroughly, slice each leek down the center, leaving the root intact, and wash well—checking between the layers for dirt.*

BLISTERED BABA GHANOUJ

I'M JUST GOING TO COME RIGHT OUT and say it: a lot of store-bought baba ghanouj can be bland and boring. And when I think about a great dip or a simple appetizer to serve with friends, I want something far from boring. So, our version of this Mediterranean favorite calls for grilling the eggplant, which gives it a nice smokiness, and then we take the flavor game one step further by using both fresh and roasted garlic. The result is a slightly sweet, supercreamy dip that I love serving as an appetizer with warm pita or crackers and crudités (or, frankly, all on its own). It's also a great filling for weekday sandwiches and wraps or slathered on bagels or flatbread.

---

8 cloves garlic, 6 left whole and 2 minced

2 teaspoons sea salt

¼ cup plus 1 tablespoon olive oil

2 large globe eggplants (firm and heavy), peeled and sliced lengthwise into ¾-inch steaks

½ cup safflower oil

¼ cup tahini

½ cup freshly squeezed lemon juice

---

1. Preheat the oven to 350°F.

2. In a small ramekin, combine the six whole garlic cloves, 1 teaspoon of the salt, and 1 tablespoon of the olive oil. Cover the ramekin with foil and bake for 25 to 30 minutes, or until the garlic is soft.

3. Lay out the eggplant steaks, brush with safflower oil, and sprinkle with the remaining teaspoon of salt. On a grill over the highest heat possible, grill each side of all the eggplant steaks for 4 to 5 minutes a side. The eggplant should have well-defined grill marks and some char. Transfer the eggplant to a baking sheet, drizzle with 2 tablespoons of the olive oil, cover with foil, and bake for 10 to 15 minutes, until very soft. Remove the foil and allow the eggplant to cool for 10 minutes at room temperature.

4. In a food processor, combine the eggplant, tahini, lemon juice, raw garlic, roasted garlic, and remaining 2 tablespoons of olive oil. Process until smooth. Allow the mixture to fully cool in the fridge before serving.

5. Serve with warm pita or vegan crackers.

CHEF'S NOTE: *When shopping for this recipe, look for a globe eggplant if you can: you want a larger, firm eggplant without any weak spots or bruises because you're going to peel, slice, and grill it. Also, if you prefer not to fire up the grill, you can broil the eggplant steaks in the oven for about 7 minutes on a sheet pan, though you will lose some of the smoky essence that really makes this dish.*

MAIN DISHES

CURRY KATSU

KATSU IS A CLASSIC JAPANESE DISH often made with chicken or tofu that's breaded in panko and fried. It's easy to find in many Japanese restaurants, but it's also pretty simple to make at home, and I hope my version gives you the necessary nudge. I've adapted this comfort food to include a fragrant curry sauce—just be sure your curry powder is no more than six months old, to ensure it's at its most flavorful. Also, start adding it in slowly: you can always add more, but it's pretty tough to take it away. At our house, we serve this katsu with Coconut Rice (page 136) but simple steamed rice or grains are great, too.

2 teaspoons sea salt

2 large carrots, peeled, sliced down the middle, and cut into ½-inch half-moons

⅔ pound Yukon Gold potatoes, cut into ½-inch chunks

2 tablespoons safflower oil

1 yellow onion, minced

1 tablespoon minced fresh ginger

2 cloves garlic, minced

¼ cup all-purpose flour

2 tablespoons curry powder

1 tablespoon tomato paste

2 tablespoons cultured shoyu

1 tablespoon vegan Worcestershire sauce

2 cups vegan vegetable stock

10 ounces full-fat coconut milk

12 ounces (about 12 pieces) Island-Style Coconut Dippers (page 32)

1. In a pot over high heat, bring 6 cups of water and the salt to a boil. Add the carrots and potatoes and boil for 4 minutes; drain and set aside.

2. In a large skillet over medium heat, heat the oil and add the onion, ginger, and garlic. Sauté the mixture, stirring occasionally, until onion is soft, 4 to 5 minutes. Add the flour and curry powder, lower the heat to low, and stir to combine. The mixture will form a roux, and will be sticky. Allow to cook, stirring occasionally, for 3 minutes. Add the tomato paste, shoyu, Worcestershire sauce, stock, and coconut milk and increase the heat to medium-high. Stirring constantly, bring the sauce to a heavy simmer as the ingredients come together. Add the potato mixture and lower the heat to a low simmer.

3. Arrange the Island-Style Coconut Dippers over Coconut Rice (page 136), steamed rice, or grains and ladle the sauce over the top.

CHEF'S NOTE: *If you can't find cultured shoyu, feel free to use soy sauce, tamari, or Bragg Liquid Aminos instead. I get shoyu at the natural foods store close to my house and like it so much because it's cultured and alive, so it's a simple way to get some healthy probiotics into my diet.*

ORANGE SZECHUAN BROCCOLI AND GRAIN MEAT

W**E HAVE A PARTY AT FIELD ROAST** every year to celebrate the Chinese New Year and this recipe quickly became a staff favorite. To be completely honest, it's my homage to mall Chinese food, which I loved as a kid but don't really eat anymore, unless I make it myself. My version has chunks of our savory meatloaf and pieces of fresh broccoli, onion, and chiles cooked down in a sweet, citrusy sauce made from marmalade, garlic, and tamari. We serve this with rice and always cross our fingers there will be leftovers for lunch the next day.

⅔ cup orange jam or marmalade

⅓ cup rice vinegar

3 cloves garlic, minced

3 tablespoons tamari

4 cups safflower or another high-heat oil, such as canola, peanut, or vegetable, for frying

1 pound Little Saigon Meatloaf (page 44) or Field Roast Classic Meatloaf, cut into 1-inch strips

⅓ cup cornstarch

2 tablespoons safflower oil

1 yellow onion, thinly sliced

2 heads broccoli, cut into bite-size florets

12 small dried Thai chilis

4 green onions, green tops sliced very thinly on the bias so they curl

1. In a saucepan, whisk together the orange jam, vinegar, garlic, and tamari over medium-low heat. Once combined, lower the heat to low and let simmer for 2 minutes. Remove from the heat and set aside.

2. In a deep fryer or Dutch oven, heat the frying oil to 375°F.

3. Toss the meatloaf chunks in cornstarch to thoroughly coat.

4. Fry in the oil for 4 minutes, or until the meat is crispy on the outside. Remove from the fryer and add to the orange sauce. Toss to coat.

5. In a skillet over medium-high heat, heat the safflower oil and add the onion. Cook until it starts to soften.

6. Add the broccoli and chiles and cover to let the broccoli steam for 2 to 3 minutes.

7. Add the meat to the vegetable mixture, garnish with green onion, and serve over rice.

ORANGE SZECHUAN BROCCOLI
AND GRAIN MEAT, PAGE 169

DAN DAN NOODLES

T HESE SZECHUAN NOODLES ARE meant to be a quick snack—think instant noodle cups, but far better and without all of those impossible-to-pronounce preservatives. A common midday or happy hour nosh, I love serving these noodles in small bowls and keeping the ingredients and method really simple. To that end, I cook the baby bok choy in the same water I cook the noodles in (fewer dishes!). You can certainly use other greens, such as broccoli or kale, if you'd prefer: just give them a quick blanch and throw them in with the noodles at the end. The red chili oil is easy to find at most Asian markets, and tahini—that supercreamy sesame paste—is a common ingredient at most well-stocked grocery stores, but feel free to use peanut butter (or your favorite nut butter) instead. Leftovers are great as an appetizer with a cold beer or, admittedly, as a most satisfying late night snack.

3 tablespoons safflower oil

¼ cup peanuts

3 tablespoons tahini

2 tablespoons chili oil with chili flakes at the bottom

1 teaspoon sesame oil

¼ cup mirin

3 tablespoons tamari

2 teaspoons sugar

2 teaspoons vegan Worcestershire sauce

¼ cup hot water

3 green onions, white portion sliced and green tops sliced very thinly on the bias so they curl

2 tablespoons ground ginger

3 cloves garlic, minced

½ pound Lemongrass and Ginger Roast (page 18) or Field Roast Lentil Sage Quarter Loaf, ground

5 ounces dried lo mein noodles

4 baby bok choy, sliced in half and cleaned

1. Line a plate with a paper towel and set aside. In a skillet or wok over medium-low heat, heat 1 tablespoon of the oil and add the peanuts. Stir occasionally until the peanuts start to become a warm brown color and look nice and toasty, about 5 minutes. Transfer these to the lined plate and set aside to cool.

2. Bring a pot of 12 cups of water to just below a boil.

3. In a small bowl, whisk together the tahini, chili oil, mirin, sesame oil, tamari, sugar, Worcestershire, and ¼ cup of hot water.

4. In a skillet or wok over medium heat, heat the remaining 2 tablespoons of oil, the white portion of the green onions, and the ginger and garlic. Sauté until the garlic becomes fragrant, then add the roast or loaf and cook, stirring occasionally, until it begins to brown, 4 to 5 minutes. Add the tahini sauce, lower the heat to medium-low, and allow to simmer.

5. While the mixture is simmering, bring the water up to a boil and add the noodles. Stir two or three times throughout the cooking process, until the noodles are fully cooked, 5 to 6 minutes. Skim or strain the noodles out, leaving the water behind in the pot at a boil. Transfer the noodles directly to the skillet of sauce, toss to combine, and lower the heat to low.

6. Add the bok choy to the boiling water and boil for 1 minute. Transfer the bok choy to a plate and set aside.

7. Roughly chop the peanuts and set aside.

8. Divide the noodles among individual bowls, serve with the bok choy, and garnish with chopped peanuts.

GINGER-GLAZED LEMONGRASS AND GINGER
ROAST WITH BLISTERED BOK CHOY, PAGE 176

GINGER-GLAZED LEMONGRASS AND GINGER ROAST WITH BLISTERED BOK CHOY

 **MAKES 4 SERVINGS**

AFTER EATING MY FAIR SHARE OF teriyaki for quick and easy lunches, I decided it was time to make a version with natural ingredients, featuring a more herbaceous (and less sweet) sauce, ramped-up sesame and ginger, and a lot of sturdy greens, such as kale, mustard greens, or radicchio. I grill the greens long enough to wilt them, and at the very end brush them with a tangy sauce. I throw the meat on the grill and continue to baste it with the glaze so it really absorbs all that sweet flavor.

¼ cup water

1 tablespoon gochujang paste (see Chef's Note)

⅓ cup light brown sugar

⅓ cup freshly squeezed lemon juice

2 tablespoons rice vinegar

¼ cup mirin

3 cloves garlic, minced

1 tablespoon minced fresh ginger

4 tablespoons sesame oil

4 tablespoons safflower oil

½ cup tamari

2 tablespoons arrowroot powder or cornstarch

1 pound Lemongrass and Ginger Roast (page 18) or Field Roast Lentil Sage Quarter Loaf, cut into thick steaks

8 baby bok choy, sliced in half and cleaned

⅓ pound fresh vegetables, such as sturdy greens or mushrooms, cleaned and left whole for grilling

1 tablespoon sesame seeds

1. In a saucepan over medium-high heat, combine the water, gochujang, brown sugar, lemon juice, vinegar, mirin, garlic, ginger, sesame oil, 2 tablespoons of safflower oil, and tamari. Stirring occasionally, bring the mixture to a boil. Add the arrowroot and whisk in. Lower the heat to low and allow the sauce to simmer for 15 to 20 minutes.

2. Brush the steaks and the bok choy with the remaining 2 tablespoons of safflower oil. Begin grilling the steaks over high heat, turning them after 3 minutes, and brushing them with the sauce. Move the steaks to a part of the grill with lower heat, or lower the heat to medium. Begin turning the steaks every 2 minutes, brushing them liberally with the sauce periodically as they cook. Remove after 8 to 10 minutes of this, and set aside.

3. While the steaks are cooking, grill the bok choy and other vegetables over high heat for 3 minutes. Set the bok choy aside, and chop the remaining vegetables into ¾-inch pieces.

4. Slice the steaks at about ½-inch thickness and serve over the vegetables. Brush the steaks with sauce again, and garnish with sesame seeds. Serve with Coconut Rice (page 136) or steamed rice.

CHEF'S NOTE: *Gochujang paste, a fermented chili paste, is a typical Korean condiment—you'll always see it on the table at Korean restaurants, and it's easy to find at Asian food markets and natural foods stores.*

TUSCAN SHEPHERD'S PIE

T HE FIELD ROAST TEAM TRAVELED to Vancouver a few years ago to participate in a Whole Foods cooking challenge where we had ninety minutes to shop for, prep, and cook a meal using one of our ingredients. I'd had shepherd's pie in mind, but the store happened to be out of a few key ingredients, so when pressed for time the dish quickly grew Italian roots as I used our Field Roast Italian Sausage (in this version, we prefer the Fennel and Garlic Sausage, page 38), fresh fennel, and mushrooms. The judges loved it and so did we. This recipe is great to make for a potluck because you can prepare it in a big baking dish and either bake it or reheat it on-site. The leftovers keep and freeze beautifully, and if you're someone who likes leftovers—like myself—this is very good news, indeed.

3 pounds Yukon Gold potatoes, peeled

5 teaspoons sea salt

½ pound mixed fresh mushrooms

7 tablespoons olive oil

2 teaspoons freshly ground black pepper

1 sprig rosemary

⅛ ounce dried porcini mushrooms

1 quart Mushroom and Herb Stock (page 196) or vegan mushroom stock

3 cloves garlic, minced

½ cup vegan butter

¼ pound vegan sour cream

4 links Fennel and Garlic Sausage (page 38) or Field Roast Italian Sausage, crumbled

2 shallots, minced

1 yellow onion, ¼-inch diced

2 carrots, ¼-inch diced

1 small to medium-size fennel bulb, ¼-inch diced

½ pound frozen English peas

2 tablespoons vegan Worcestershire sauce

Leaves from 4 sprigs dill, minced

1. Preheat the oven to 450°F.

2. In a large stockpot over high heat, bring 5 quarts of water to a boil. Add the potatoes, along with 1 tablespoon of the salt. Cover and allow to cook for 25 minutes over high heat, or until the potatoes are soft all the way through. Drain the potatoes, and allow to sit while you start the rest of the dish.

3. Brush the dirt off the fresh mushrooms, slice, and coat with 2 tablespoons of the oil, 1½ teaspoons of the remaining salt, and 1 teaspoon of the pepper. Place on a sheet pan along with the rosemary and roast in the oven for 10 minutes, or until browned. Remove the rosemary, combine the roasted mushrooms with mushroom stock and porcini mushrooms in a stockpot over medium heat, and allow to reduce for 25 to 30 minutes. Using an immersion blender, puree the mixture into a gravy and set aside.

continues on page 178

4. In a large mixing bowl, combine half of the garlic with the potato, butter, ½ teaspoon salt, and sour cream. Mash with a large whisk or potato masher.

5. In a skillet over medium heat, heat 3 tablespoons of the oil, add the crumbled sausage, and sauté to lightly brown the sausage.

6. Add the remaining garlic, shallot, onion, carrot, fennel, 1 teaspoon of pepper, and 2 tablespoons oil, and sauté until the onion is translucent. Once vegetables have cooked down, lower the heat and allow to simmer, while adding half of the gravy mixture, the peas, and the Worcestershire sauce. Allow to reduce until almost all the liquid is gone.

7. In a baking dish, spread the sausage mixture across the bottom, then top with the potato mixture. Bake for 25 to 30 minutes, removing from the oven when the potato on top has begun to brown. Before serving, ladle a small amount of the remaining gravy onto a serving plate, then place the pie on top and garnish with dill.

MOFONGOS

I DISCOVERED THIS POPULAR mashed plantain dish while traveling in Puerto Rico and have made it dozens of times since, constantly perfecting and tweaking. Traditionally made with underripe green plantains mashed with garlic and butter, mofongos are formed into a ramekin and baked so they're nice and crisp on the outside. As if they weren't delicious enough as they are, I take these one step further by turning them into more of a relleno: pressing the plantain mixture into the ramekin, making a little divot in the middle for a filling, covering it with plantain, and baking it. You want to serve these guys hot, right out of the oven, preferably with cold beer or an iced rum cocktail.

---

3 tablespoons olive oil

½ medium-size yellow onion, minced

1 chipotle pepper in adobo, minced, with 2 tablespoons adobo sauce

4 cloves garlic, minced

1 bay leaf

3 teaspoons sea salt

2 teaspoons ground cumin

2 teaspoons chili powder

1 (4-ounce) can green chiles, drained

¾ pound Lemongrass and Ginger Roast (page 18) or Field Roast Lentil Sage Quarter Loaf, cut into ½-inch cubes

Leaves from 2 sprigs oregano

¾ cup vegan vegetable stock

10 ounces cherry tomatoes, halved

2 to 3 cups safflower or another high-heat oil, such as canola, peanut, or vegetable, for frying, plus more for brushing (optional)

4 green plantains

¼ cup vegan butter

Safflower or canola oil spray (optional)

4 sprigs cilantro, large stems removed, roughly chopped

---

1. In a skillet over medium heat, heat the olive oil and add the onion, chipotle pepper, half of the garlic, the bay leaf, 1 teaspoon of the salt, and the cumin and chili powder. Using a wooden spoon, stir to combine. Allow to cook, stirring occasionally, for 5 to 7 minutes, or until the onion begins to become translucent. Add the chiles, roast or loaf, oregano, and vegetable stock and stir. Lower the heat to low and allow the mixture to simmer and reduce, stirring occasionally, until most of the liquid has been absorbed, 8 to 10 minutes. Remove from the heat, add the tomatoes, stir to combine, and set aside.

2. In a deep fryer or Dutch oven, heat the frying oil to 350°F.

3. Peel the plantains and slice into 1-inch rounds. Fry the plantains until golden and tender, 5 to 6 minutes, and transfer to a paper towel–lined plate. Using a mortar and pestle, mash the plantains, vegan butter, remaining garlic, and remaining 2 teaspoons of salt until the mixture starts to resemble chunky mashed potatoes. Taste and adjust for salt.

4. Preheat the oven to 425°F.

5. Spray or brush four medium-size oven-safe bowls or ramekins with oil, divide the mixture into four equal portions, and place into the bowls. Using a spoon or your hands, press the plantain mixture out toward the sides of each bowl, creating a pocket in the middle. Spoon some of the roast mixture into the pocket and push the sides of the plantain mixture over the filling, creating a plantain top.

6. Transfer the bowls to the oven and bake for 15 minutes. The plantains on top will start to brown. Remove from the oven and garnish with cilantro.

COCHINITA PIBIL

THIS CLASSIC MEXICAN DISH IS usually made with pork. My cochinita pibil is made with jackfruit, which, after an hour or two of cooking, takes on the texture and flavor of pulled pork. I season it and roast it in banana leaves to keep it from drying out and really give the flavors a chance to intensify. After getting some pickled onions all set, I serve the savory shredded jackfruit on the banana leaves themselves, with a few warm tortillas on the side. A great recipe for a crowd, you can set it all out on a platter and friends can make little tacos and stand and snack as they please.

---

2 teaspoons sea salt

½ cup red wine vinegar

1 tablespoon sugar

1 small red onion, thinly sliced into half-moons

6 to 8 chiles de árbol, stems removed

3 tablespoons olive oil

3 cloves garlic, minced

½ teaspoon ground cinnamon

1 tablespoon ground cumin

½ teaspoon ground cloves

2 teaspoons black peppercorns

Leaves from 4 sprigs oregano

¼ cup freshly squeezed lime juice

1 tablespoon safflower oil

2 (20-ounce) cans young jackfruit, drained

1 banana leaf, cut into 2 (9 x 12-inch) rectangles (see Chef's Note)

---

1. In a small saucepan over medium heat, combine 1 teaspoon of the salt and the vinegar and sugar. Stir until the salt and sugar dissolve, remove from the heat, and add the red onion; stir to coat. Transfer the pickled onions to a bowl and chill in the fridge.

2. Place the chiles in a small bowl or heat-safe container and pour in enough boiling water to cover. Cover the container and allow to steep for 5 minutes.

3. Preheat the oven to 300°F.

4. In a pan over low heat, heat 1 tablespoon of the olive oil and add the garlic, cinnamon, cumin, clove, peppercorns, and chiles (reserve the liquid). Toast the spices, stirring occasionally, for 5 to 7 minutes, or until they become fragrant. Transfer the mixture to a blender and add the remaining teaspoon of salt, the oregano and lime juice, the remaining 2 tablespoons of olive oil, and ¼ cup of the liquid used to steep the chiles. Blend until smooth.

5. In a skillet over medium heat, heat the safflower oil and add the jackfruit. Stir this mixture occasionally so it doesn't stick to the bottom of the pan. The liquid will begin cooking out of the jackfruit and it will become soft enough to press it apart, using your spoon. Press the large chunks of jackfruit apart and add the spice mixture from the blender. Allow this to cook down, as the jackfruit absorbs the spices, and it begins to "shred" and resemble pulled pork, 10 to 15 minutes. Remove from the heat.

6. Lay out both sections of the banana leaf so that they overlap in the middle and form a cross. Transfer the jackfruit to the middle and fold the leaves into a pouch. Transfer the pouch to a baking dish or sheet pan and bake for 40 minutes.

7. Remove the pouch from the baking dish and unwrap on a platter or large plate. Serve with warm tortillas and the pickled onions.

CHEF'S NOTE: *Banana leaves should be readily available at most Asian or Mexican grocery stores.*

COCHINITA PIBIL, PAGE 182

SMOKY KALUA JACKFRUIT

THE SUPERSTAR OF OUR Hawaiian Plate Lunch, this smoky jackfruit is the vegan version of a pork dish that's typically buried underground in banana leaves and roasted. Here I use our Mushroom and Herb Roast instead of pork and some mushroom stock and liquid smoke to cook the jackfruit down and flavor it—the result is a really rich, intense umami flavor combined with a little brown sugar and ginger for some subtle sweetness. To learn more about *umami*, see page 19. As the jackfruit cooks, be sure to continue mashing it down with a spoon so it gets that nice, shredded texture you want. Beyond the Hawaiian lunch, the jackfruit is great in wraps, as part of a sandwich with some BBQ sauce, or folded into your favorite chili recipe.

---

1 tablespoon safflower oil

6 cloves garlic, minced

1 tablespoon minced fresh ginger

½ cup tamari

2 teaspoons liquid smoke

2 tablespoons dark brown sugar

¼ cup Mushroom and Herb Stock (page 196) or vegan mushroom stock

2 (20-ounce) cans young jackfruit, drained

2 ounces Mushroom and Herb Roast (page 24) or Field Roast Wild Mushroom Quarter Loaf or Deli Slices, sliced into small, thin strips

---

1. Preheat the oven to 350°F.

2. In a small pan over medium heat, heat the safflower oil and add the garlic and ginger. Sauté, stirring occasionally, for 5 minutes, until the garlic and ginger become fragrant. Transfer to a baking dish.

3. Add the tamari, liquid smoke, brown sugar, and mushroom stock to the baking dish and stir to combine. Add the jackfruit and toss to fully coat. Cover the baking dish with foil and bake for 40 minutes.

4. After 40 minutes in the oven, transfer the jackfruit and any liquid to a skillet over medium heat. Add the roast and stir the mixture to combine. Allow this mixture to cook, stirring occasionally, until the liquid is absorbed and the jackfruit begins to shred and become crispy. As you stir, use your spoon to mash the jackfruit and break it into shred-type pieces. After 10 to 15 minutes, remove from the heat and serve.

SERVING SUGGESTION: *Serve the jackfruit with Macaroni Salad (page 120), Lomi Lomi Salad (page 119), and steamed rice for a delicious plate lunch (see photo page 118).*

GRILLED PIZZA SALCHICHA

E VERY YEAR WE HAVE A FIELD DAY at Field Roast, when the staff heads outdoors to enjoy a little friendly competition and grilled pizza. I'm seeing a lot of home pizza ovens and pizza stones
in the food magazines lately, but really all you need to make a killer pizza at home is a basic grill. The
thing to know here is you're going to put these on the grill twice: the first time to par-grill the dough
so it's firm, and the second time you'll add your sauce and toppings and put it on the grill again to
warm the toppings and melt the cheese. Once you get the hang of these, having a pizza party at home
is a great excuse to have friends over and fire up the grill: simply par-grill a bunch of crusts, lay out
seasonal toppings, and everyone can get down to business. While I call for Kite Hill soft cheese here,
any vegan brand will work just fine. Likewise, use any vegetables or toppings that inspire you—it's
hard to go wrong.

---

3 tablespoons vegan butter

Leaves from 2 sprigs thyme

2 teaspoons sea salt

½ pound mushrooms (oyster, chanterelle,
shiitake, or whatever combination you
prefer), cleaned with a brush or towel
and sliced

2 cloves garlic, minced

2 tablespoons blanched almonds, chopped
into a coarse meal

3 sprigs dill, large stems removed, roughly
chopped

Leaves from 4 sprigs oregano

2 ounces (about 2 cups) fresh basil leaves,
stems removed

⅓ cup plus ¼ cup olive oil

All-purpose flour, for dusting

1 pound Slow Poke Pizza Dough (page 200)
or your favorite vegan pizza dough,
removed from fridge about 1 hour before
you plan to grill

7 ounces Fennel and Garlic Sausage
(page 38) or Field Roast Italian Sausage,
crumbled

¼ cup pickled peppers (I like Mama Lil's)

3 to 4 ounces favorite soft vegan cheese
(I like to use Kite Hill for this)

---

1. In a saucepan over medium-high heat, melt the butter and add the thyme, 1 teaspoon of the salt,
and the mushrooms. Sauté, stirring occasionally, for 10 to 15 minutes, or until the mushrooms are
soft and begin to brown. Transfer to a plate and set aside.

2. In a blender or food processor, combine the garlic, almonds, dill, oregano, remaining teaspoon of
salt, basil, and ⅓ cup of the olive oil. Puree until it creates a smooth pesto.

3. Sprinkle a little flour on a work surface and roll out your dough into one or multiple portions.
Brush the dough on both sides with a liberal amount of the remaining ¼ cup of olive oil. On a grill
over high heat, stretch out the oiled dough until the portions are almost translucent. Allow the dough
to cook for 2 to 3 minutes, or until the crust is rigid enough to flip. Then, flip the crust, grill for a few

seconds, then transfer to a board with the crust's most grilled side up. Spread on some of the pesto, followed by the sausage, mushrooms, peppers, and vegan cheese. Return the crust to the grill to cook for another 3 to 4 minutes. Remove from the grill, slice, and serve immediately.

CHEF'S NOTE: *To avoid having your pizza stick to the grill, make sure to brush the grates with oil as well as both sides of your dough, and make sure your grill is nice and hot.*

MAIN DISHES

★

187

PAELLA

A GREAT PARTY DISH AND ONE OF my favorite things to cook on my birthday, paella is a one-pot, flavor-packed rice dish that's easy to customize and tailor to your preference. We often dress ours up, slicing king trumpet mushrooms and grilling sausage to serve on top—the mushrooms look a lot like scallops and have a great, meaty texture and flavor. You can treat this recipe as a bit of a template in the sense that any vegetables will fly—use whatever's in season or easily on hand. I would recommend serving the paella outdoors if the weather permits, preferably with a crisp vinho verde or rosé—or a cold glass of beer.

3½ cups vegan vegetable stock

¼ cup olive oil

1 yellow onion

5 cloves garlic, minced

2 carrots, peeled and ¼-inch diced

Large pinch of saffron threads

2 teaspoons smoked paprika

1 yellow bell pepper, cut into strips

1 red bell pepper, cut into strips

3 king trumpet mushrooms, cleaned, stems cut into ¾-inch rounds and tops sliced

½ cup white wine

1 teaspoon sea salt, plus more for seasoning

1½ cups Arborio rice

2 links Oaxacan Chili-Spiced Sausage (page 42) or Field Roast Mexican Chipotle Sausage

3 firm, on-the-vine tomatoes, sliced in half

1 teaspoon freshly ground black pepper

Leaves from 6 sprigs parsley, roughly chopped

1 cup English peas

1 lemon, sliced into wedges

1. In a pan over high heat, bring the stock to a boil, then lower the heat to low.

2. In a medium-size paella pan or large skillet over medium heat, heat the oil and add the onion, garlic, carrot, saffron, and paprika. Sauté the mixture, stirring occasionally, for 7 minutes. Add the bell peppers, sliced mushroom tops, wine, salt, and rice. Stir to combine, then sauté, stirring occasionally, for another 5 minutes.

3. Pour the stock over the rice and increase the heat to high. Bring the rice to a boil, then lower the heat to low, while stirring. Cover the pan with foil and allow the rice to cook over low heat for 18 minutes, then turn off the heat. Leaving the foil on the pan, allow the rice to steam with no heat for another 15 minutes.

continues on page 190

4. While the rice is cooking, brush the sausage, mushroom stem rounds, and tomatoes with oil, and top with additional salt and black pepper. Grill over high heat. The tomatoes will take about 5 minutes, and should only be grilled on the flat side. The sausage and mushrooms will take about 8 minutes, and should be turned halfway through. Remove the items from the grill, slice the sausage, and cut the tomatoes into quarters.

5. Remove the cover from the paella and arrange the sausage, mushrooms, and tomatoes on top. Garnish with the parsley, peas, and lemon wedges.

CHEF'S NOTE: *No paella pan at home? A large skillet will work fine—ultimately you just need something that's large and shallow.*

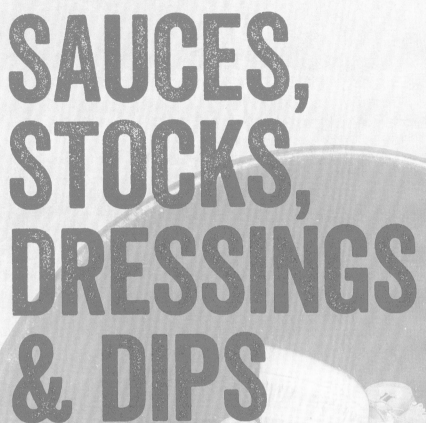

SAUCES, STOCKS, DRESSINGS & DIPS

VEGAN BÉCHAMEL

WHENEVER A RECIPE CALLS FOR a heavy cream sauce, our vegan béchamel is an obvious substitute. A pantry staple around the Field Roast kitchen for good reason, this supercreamy sauce was inspired by a few friends who run a plant-based website called Wicked Healthy. What makes it different from other vegan sauces? It relies on boiled garlic for flavor, which may seem slightly fussy at first, but boiling it actually removes the sharpness and replaces it with mellow, almost sweet, creamy layers of flavor. I love this sauce on pastas and whole-grain dishes or drizzled over roasted vegetables, and we use it as a base for a number of the recipes in this book.

8 cloves garlic, left whole

1 cup raw cashews

2 teaspoons safflower oil

½ yellow onion, ¼-inch diced

¼ cup white wine

2½ cups water, plus more if needed

3 tablespoons nutritional yeast

1 tablespoon white miso

2 teaspoons onion powder

1 teaspoon smoked paprika

½ teaspoon ground nutmeg

1 teaspoon mustard powder

2 teaspoons Dijon mustard

2 teaspoons sea salt

1. In a small saucepan filled with water, boil the garlic for 5 minutes. Drain and set aside.

2. In a medium-size bowl, cover the cashews with ample water and soak for 2 hours. Drain them and transfer to a blender.

3. In a medium-size saucepan over medium heat, heat the oil and add the onion. Cook the onion until it begins to soften and glisten. Add the wine and lower the heat to low. Allow to simmer for 3 to 4 minutes, or until most of the moisture is gone. Remove from the heat and add to the blender.

4. Add the remaining ingredients, including the 2½ cups of water, to the blender and process until very smooth, adding more water, if needed. The result should be the consistency of a melted milk shake. You can freeze any extra for later use in a gallon-size resealable plastic bag for up to 6 months.

VEGAN HOLLANDAISE

WHEN MY GRANDMOTHER on my dad's side learned that I might want to cook for a living, she promptly quizzed me on the mother sauces. After all, she'd say, all good cooks know the mother sauces. And while I couldn't necessarily rattle them off at the time, they've become a deeply ingrained part of the recipes in my arsenal today. This hollandaise is probably the one I look to the most, and it's special because it manages to be vegan and supercreamy. It's incredible on our Florentine Benedict (page 61) and you can easily turn it into a béarnaise sauce by adding a little vinegar, tarragon, and shallot.

1½ cups unsweetened plain almond milk

1 tablespoon Follow Your Heart vegan egg

3 tablespoons vegan butter

1 tablespoon all-purpose flour

3 tablespoons freshly squeezed lemon juice

1 teaspoon sea salt

2 tablespoons vegan mayo

1 pinch of cayenne pepper

1. In a blender, combine the milk and vegan egg.

2. In a saucepan over medium heat, melt the butter, then add the flour, whisking until the mixture is fully combined. Slowly add the milk, a little at a time, while whisking, allowing the temperature to come back up to a heavy simmer. When all the milk mixture is fully incorporated, lower heat to low. Add the lemon juice, salt, mayo, and cayenne and whisk together. The mixture should be silky and pourable. You can adjust the thickness by adding more milk to thin, or more mayo to thicken, to your desired result. This sauce tends to separate when frozen, so I don't recommend saving it for later.

THE SAUCE BBQ SAUCE

 **MAKES ABOUT 4 CUPS**

THERE ARE A LOT OF STRONG OPINIONS when it comes to homemade barbecue sauce. Let's face it: it can be a pretty divisive topic. My recipe is a true Texas pit sauce, with a nice balanced flavor and a good vinegar bite—but not thick and sweet like many of the bottled varieties you'll find. I only use one chipotle pepper here, so if you like yours spicier, feel free to add another. In the warmer months, I make a double batch of this sauce and freeze half, so we're always prepared to get the grill going and settle into a good Seattle summer night.

1 tablespoon vegan butter

4 cloves garlic, minced

½ medium-size yellow onion, minced

1 tablespoon chili powder

2 teaspoons ground cumin

1 cup Mushroom and Herb Stock (page 196) or vegan mushroom stock

1 (15-ounce) can tomato sauce

1 chipotle pepper in adobo with 1 tablespoon of adobo sauce

½ cup cider vinegar

½ cup dark brown sugar

2 teaspoons freshly ground black pepper

½ teaspoon liquid smoke

1 tablespoon vegan Worcestershire sauce

1 tablespoon sea salt

1. In a saucepan over medium-high heat, melt the butter and add the garlic, onion, chili powder, and cumin. Stirring occasionally, sauté for 8 to 10 minutes, until the onion is translucent and beginning to brown. Lower the heat to medium-low and add the remaining ingredients. Allow the sauce to simmer for 30 to 40 minutes, until it has thickened and become glossy. Remove from the heat and blend with an immersion blender. Chill in the fridge overnight.

CHEF'S NOTE: *To freeze the sauce, make sure you let it cool all the way and divide it among small resealable plastic freezer bags, laying them flat in the freezer.*

LEMONGRASS AND GINGER STOCK

I USE THIS LIGHT, FLAVOR-PACKED, versatile recipe in our roasts and as a base for many of our soups. It's a great substitute whenever chicken stock is called for, and is far cheaper and more flavorful than any store-bought brand. For that reason, I often make a double batch and freeze it, so we always have it at the ready. While I love the flavor of this stock, don't feel too married to the recipe itself: feel free to deviate from it, treating it more like a template rather than a hard-and-fast formula—after all, a good stock can be made using many combinations of vegetable trimmings (carrot tops, onion skins, or the top and bottoms of celery, to name just a few, avoiding strong bitter greens or root vegetables). I keep a bag of scraps in my freezer and just continue to add to it until I have enough to make a decent pot of stock.

2 carrots, roughly chopped	4 sprigs thyme
1 yellow onion, roughly chopped	4 bay leaves
4 stalks celery, roughly chopped	1 tablespoon black peppercorns
1 large leek, roughly chopped	1 tablespoon sea salt
1 clove garlic, sliced down the middle	2 tablespoons safflower oil
1 stalk lemongrass, pounded with the back of a chef's knife (see page 9)	1 tablespoon sesame oil
	⅔ cup tamari or soy sauce
1 large piece kombu	14 cups water

1. Preheat the oven to 450°F.

2. In a large bowl, combine all the ingredients, except the safflower oil, sesame oil, tamari, and water. Toss the ingredients to thoroughly coat with the safflower oil and arrange on a sheet pan. Roast in the oven for 20 minutes, stirring occasionally. The ingredients should have begun to caramelize and turn brown.

3. Place the roasted mixture in a large stockpot and add the sesame oil, tamari, and water. Over high heat, bring to a boil, then reduce the heat to medium and simmer, covered, for about 2 hours. Remove from the heat and allow to cool uncovered.

4. When the stock has cooled for about 2 hours, strain out the vegetables and transfer the liquid, to a depth of no more than 2 inches deep, to a large dish or high-capacity container that will fit in your fridge, and chill in the fridge.

5. Once cool, the stock can be frozen in a freezer-safe container for 6 months.

MUSHROOM AND HERB STOCK

U MAMI IS THE NAME OF THE GAME HERE, and we use fresh and dried mushrooms as well as kombu to really ramp up this deep, rich, fragrant stock. While there isn't a lot of technique involved in making a good stock, I do have one trick up my sleeve: I love roasting the vegetables before working with them, as it gives the recipe more depth and imparts a lot of caramelized flavor that makes for big, bold flavors. Use any mushrooms you like here, but be sure to clean them dry, with a brush, instead of using water. Mushrooms are porous, so they'll absorb all that water, which will change the way they cook and react. As for the dried mushrooms, if you can get to an Asian supermarket, they'll be far cheaper and often come in larger packages. Then there's an even greater chance that there will always be homemade stock in your future.

---

2 carrots, roughly chopped

1 yellow onion, roughly chopped

¾ pound mixed fresh mushrooms, roughly chopped

1 clove garlic, sliced down the middle

2 tablespoons tomato paste

1 leek, cleaned well and roughly chopped

1 piece kombu

1 sprig rosemary

4 sprigs thyme

3 sprigs oregano

4 bay leaves

1 tablespoon black peppercorns

1 tablespoon sea salt

2 tablespoons safflower oil

14 cups water

¼ ounce dried mushrooms

---

1. Preheat the oven to 450°F.

2. In a large bowl, combine all the ingredients, except the water and dried mushrooms. Mix thoroughly to coat with the oil and tomato paste, and arrange on a sheet pan.

3. Roast in the preheated oven, stirring occasionally. The mixture should have begun to caramelize and turn brown.

4. Transfer the mixture to a large stockpot, add the water and dried mushrooms, and bring to a boil. Lower the heat to medium, cover, and allow to simmer for 2 hours. Remove from the heat, and allow to cool uncovered.

5. When the stock has cooled for about 2 hours, strain out the vegetables and transfer the liquid, to a depth of no more than 2 inches deep, to a large dish or high-capacity container that will fit in your fridge, and chill in the fridge.

6. Once cool, the stock can be frozen in a freezer-safe container for 6 months.

FRESH JUICED CURRY DRESSING

Abright and juicy marinade or a superlight dressing, we use this vibrant recipe on our Laotian Citrus Salad (page 108), but I find myself craving it on all my salads in the dead of winter when, let's face it, Seattleites desperately crave color wherever we can get it. The lemon, ginger, and carrot compose much of the flavor, but really, it's all about the curry. I use a high-speed blender (such as a Vitamix) to pull this together because it actually heats up while blending, which helps open up the oils and intense flavor in the curry powder. Because it relies on fruits and vegetables instead of a lot of oil, it's lower in fat and will therefore separate after a day or so in the fridge, so just give it a good shake to bring it back together.

6 cloves garlic, left whole

½ carrot, peeled and cut into large chunks

½ pear, peeled and cored

2 tablespoons curry powder

3 tablespoons freshly squeezed lemon juice

1 tablespoon minced fresh ginger

½ cup seasoned rice vinegar

3 tablespoons olive or avocado oil

Leaves from 3 sprigs mint

1 tablespoon sriracha

2 teaspoons agave syrup

2 teaspoons sea salt

½ cup water

1. In a small saucepan filled with water, boil the garlic for 5 minutes until soft. Drain and set aside.

2. In a high-speed blender, combine all the remaining ingredients plus the boiled garlic. Blend on high speed until the pitcher becomes warm to the touch and the mixture has turned yellow. Taste and adjust for salt.

3. If you do not have a high-speed blender: Using a regular blender, place the boiled garlic cloves, while still hot, in the blender along with the oil and curry powder, and blend together first. This will make the curry more fragrant. Afterward, add the remaining ingredients and blend until smooth, about 3 minutes.

CHEF'S NOTES: *Any variety of pear will work in this dressing. If your pear is very ripe and sweet, you may want to omit the agave syrup.*

AVOCADO RANCH DRESSING

IN MY LIMITED POLLING, IT SEEMS that ranch dressing is a guilty pleasure for many people, myself included. So, how about a ranch dressing you can feel good about instead of one filled with hydrogenated oil and sodium? For this recipe, I replaced a lot of the oil with avocado, and in doing so worked in all those healthy monounsaturated fats and fiber. Not that you'll need suggestions for what to do with this supercreamy and addictive dressing, I will say it's the perfect accompaniment to our Spicy Corn and Chili Fritters (page 152), makes a great veggie dip, and turns even the most humble salad into something special.

1 avocado, peeled, pitted, and quartered	12 sprigs chives, minced
1 cup vegan mayo	1 clove garlic, minced
¼ cup white vinegar	4 sprigs dill, large stems removed, minced
3 tablespoons freshly squeezed lemon juice	2 teaspoons onion powder
1 tablespoon vegan Worcestershire sauce	2 teaspoons sea salt

1. Place all the ingredients in a food processor and blend until smooth.

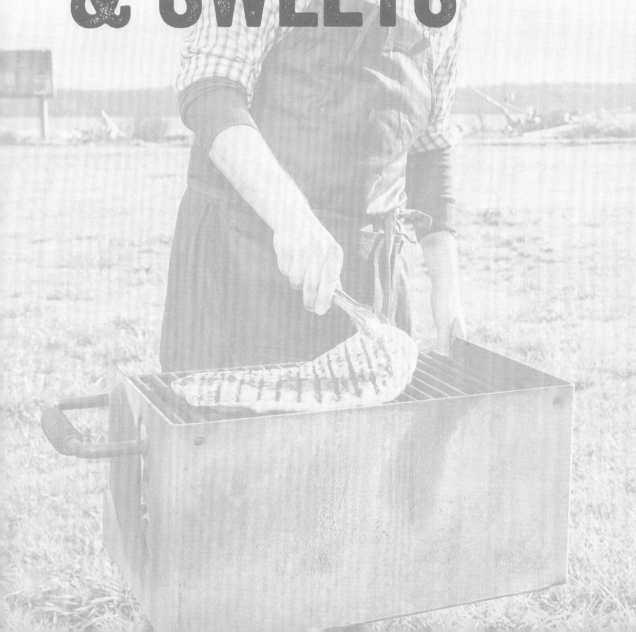

BREADS & SWEETS

SLOW POKE PIZZA DOUGH

 **MAKES 1 POUND**

PIZZA DOUGH IS ONE OF THOSE things that's not at all difficult to make at home and actually tastes infinitely better than store-bought. Personally, I like my pizza dough to have some character, so I use a real yeast starter, but most people don't keep their own starter at home, so I've improvised here—essentially creating a poor man's sourdough and allowing you to capture that same depth of flavor with a can of beer! And really, an inexpensive lager, such as PBR or Rainier (a Seattle favorite), is the very best. Once you make this dough once, chances are it'll be in heavy rotation: it's superversatile and great for pizza, flatbreads, breadsticks, or calzones. Do know that it requires time to rest in the fridge before baking, so plan accordingly.

3½ cups all-purpose flour, plus more for sprinkling

¼ ounce active dry yeast

1 teaspoon sugar

½ cup water warm (about 80°F)

1 cup cheap lager beer, such as Rainier or PBR

1 teaspoon sea salt

¼ cup olive oil, plus more for brushing bowl

EQUIPMENT

Stand mixer with a dough hook

1. In a stand mixer fitted with a dough hook, combine ¼ cup of the flour, yeast, sugar, and warm water. Whisk well and sprinkle a small amount of flour on top. Let sit for about 15 minutes.

2. After 15 minutes, you should see the flour start to "crack" on the top (if you don't, just wait a little longer).

3. Add the remaining ingredients, and set the mixer on low speed for 10 to 15 minutes. The dough should come together to form a ball and come away from the sides of the bowl.

4. Transfer the dough to a clean mixing bowl with high sides, brushed with a small amount of oil. Cover and chill the bowl in the fridge for at least 8 hours, but no more than 20 hours. At this point, the dough should have doubled in size. If it has not, place your dough in a room-temperature spot and allow it to finish rising. Using your hands, punch down the dough and form it into a ball. Before using, allow the dough to come up to just below room temperature.

5. The dough should be used within 2 days and can be kept wrapped in the fridge.

GENESEE BISCUITS

M OST VEGAN BISCUITS I'VE tried either come up short in the flavor or flakiness department (or both), so I'm really proud that these taste just like down-home fluffy beauties. While initially it may seem odd, it's no mistake that I call for vegan butter and Earth Balance Buttery Spread here: they each work together to create height and layers. To form the biscuits, I use a biscuit cutter or a ring, although an aluminum can would work just fine, too. Be sure to push all the way down and then twist to cut the biscuit—don't twist while you're pushing or you'll affect the layers and, ultimately, the flakiness. I use these biscuits for Biscuits and Gravy (page 55) and they're also wonderful as the base for a seasonal shortcake or trifle.

---

2 cups all-purpose flour, plus more for rolling

1 tablespoon baking powder

¼ teaspoon baking soda

1 teaspoon sea salt

1 cup unsweetened plain almond milk

1 tablespoon Follow Your Heart vegan egg

2 teaspoons freshly squeezed lemon juice

¼ cup water

3 tablespoons vegan butter, cut into ½-inch chunks and chilled

¼ cup Earth Balance Buttery Spread, cut into ½-inch chunks and chilled

---

1. Preheat the oven to 375°F.

2. Whisk together the flour, baking powder, baking soda, and salt.

3. In a blender, blend together the milk and vegan egg. Set ¼ cup of the mixture aside. To the rest of the milk mixture, add the lemon juice and water; stir to combine.

4. In a food processor, or using a pastry cutter, cut the butter and Earth Balance into the flour mixture, until the chunks of butter are the size of small pebbles. Turn this out into a large mixing bowl. Pour the acidified milk mixture into the flour mixture, and mix until combined. Turn out the dough onto a floured surface and knead, folding the dough over itself four times. Using a floured rolling pin, roll out the dough into a 1-inch-thick rectangle. Using a biscuit cutter or ring, cut the biscuits by pushing down and then twisting.

5. Transfer the biscuits to a parchment paper– or a silicone mat–lined baking sheet and brush with the reserved milk mixture. Bake for 20 minutes, or until the biscuits just begin to brown. Remove from the baking sheet and allow to cool on a rack.

CHEF'S NOTE: *When you roll and cut these the first time, you're going to have a little extra dough. Reroll and recut a second time, but don't do it a third time, or else your biscuits will start to become tough and you'll lose those coveted layers.*

FRESH HERB FOCACCIA

 **MAKES 1 LOAF**

I F YOU SHY AWAY FROM BAKING because you worry you'll mess up the appearance of a layer cake or can't form the perfect scone, you're in luck: this focaccia is meant to be dimply and uneven and imperfect. It's meant to be lumpy on top with lots of good texture. This recipe makes a great panino, a trusty sidekick to a hearty soup or stew, and is my go-to for the Strata Provençal (page 62).

STARTER

¼ teaspoon instant yeast

½ cup warm water (100°F)

½ cup all-purpose flour

DOUGH

1 cup warm water

1 teaspoon instant yeast

1 tablespoon sea salt, plus more for sprinkling on top

2½ cups all-purpose flour

1 cup olive oil

Leaves from 3 sprigs thyme

Leaves from 3 sprigs oregano

Leaves from 1 sprig rosemary

⅓ cup kalamata olives, chopped

EQUIPMENT

Stand mixer

1. For the starter: In a large bowl, combine the yeast, water, and flour and stir until fully mixed. Cover with plastic wrap and leave at room temperature overnight.

2. The next day, transfer the starter to a stand mixer fitted with a dough hook and add the warm water, yeast, salt, and flour. Mix on medium speed for 7 minutes, then add ½ cup of the oil and continue to mix until the dough comes together. Transfer the dough to a floured surface and begin kneading. Knead for an additional 7 to 8 minutes. Add the herbs and olives and continue to knead until the herbs are distributed throughout. If at any point the dough becomes too sticky, sprinkle with additional flour and continue to knead until you have a smooth dough. Return the dough to the mixing bowl and cover with a towel. Allow the dough to rise for 90 minutes, or until it has doubled in size.

3. Meanwhile, preheat the oven to 425°F. On a lightly floured surface, begin to stretch the dough into a rectangular shape that will fit a baking sheet. Pour the remaining ½ cup of oil onto the pan and transfer the dough to the pan. Stretch the dough to the corners, using your fingers. The dough should be rough looking, and if your fingers poke through, it will only help to add texture to the finished bread. When you have stretched the bread to the corners, flip it over to coat the other side with oil. Sprinkle the top lightly with salt. Place the pan on the middle rack of your oven.

5. Bake the bread for 30 minutes, or until golden brown. Remove from the oven and allow to cool.

CHEF'S NOTE: *Do plan ahead here, as the recipe needs to pre-ferment to give it a nice, deep flavor. It will require a day to sit before actually baking.*

VANILLA RHUBARB HAND
TARTS, PAGE 204

VANILLA RHUBARB HAND TARTS

I'VE NEVER BEEN ONE FOR FUSSY, incredibly refined desserts, always preferring a rustic hand tart any day of the week. And rhubarb is one of my favorite ingredients to bake with, so these are right up my alley. People often seem to feel the need to pair rhubarb with something else, as if you need to swoop in and save it, but in reality the tart stalks need very little to accompany them. This filling is a simple mixture of the vibrant rhubarb—which I par-roast to remove some of the moisture— a little sugar, lemon juice, and lots of vanilla bean. The dough is very similar to a pie dough except I use a good bit of vegan cream cheese to make it supereasy to handle and roll out. Each tart will be a little irregular, so don't feel the need to make these perfect: they can be wonky and are all the more delicious for it. Serve with coconut whipped cream, ice cream, or a good cup of coffee at the end of a meal. And I have to admit that they make a pretty fine breakfast the next morning, too.

CRUST

6 tablespoons vegan butter, cut into chunks and chilled

1½ cups all-purpose flour, plus more for dusting

1 teaspoon salt

2 teaspoons sugar

¼ cup cold water

¼ cup vegan cream cheese, cut into chunks and chilled

FILLING

2 pounds rhubarb, sliced into ½-inch slices

1 cup sugar

4 vanilla beans, sliced down the middle and seeds scraped out for use

¼ cup freshly squeezed lemon juice

WASH

¼ cup unsweetened plain almond milk

1. Prepare the crust first: In a food processor, combine the butter, flour, salt, and sugar. Pulse until it resembles coarse cornmeal. Add the cold water and cream cheese and pulse a few more times until the ingredients have been combined; the mixture may still be a little loose. Transfer the mixture to a floured board and mix once more with your hands. Wrap the dough in plastic wrap and chill for 1 hour.

2. Meanwhile, heat the oven to 425°F.

3. In a large mixing bowl, combine the rhubarb, sugar, vanilla seeds, and lemon juice, stirring well. Transfer the mixture to a baking sheet and roast in the oven for 10 minutes. Remove from the oven and let cool.

4. Once the mixture is cool, remove your dough from the fridge. Unwrap the dough and knead it once or twice on a board. If the dough is still a little loose, you may sprinkle it with a little water to help bring it together. Divide the dough into 1½-inch balls. On a floured board, using a rolling pin, roll out the balls until each is 3½ to 4 inches in diameter. Place about ¼ cup of the rhubarb mixture onto the middle of each dough round, and begin folding the edges in and over the filling, leaving a small opening in the middle. These are meant to be hand formed and a little rustic looking, so don't worry if they all look a little different. I start by folding an edge inward, and then begin moving around the dough round, folding a little bit of dough back onto the edge I just created until I have made it all the way around.

5. Brush each tart with a little bit of the milk wash (you can also sprinkle with some additional sugar), and transfer to a parchment paper– or silicone mat–lined baking sheet. Bake for 20 minutes, or until the crust starts to brown. Remove from the oven and allow to cool on a rack or plate.

6. To make ahead, the tarts can be frozen on a baking sheet while still raw and kept in the freezer for up to 6 months. Fully thaw before following the above baking instructions.

RED, WHITE, AND BLUEBERRY SHORTCAKE

WHEN I WAS A LITTLE KID, the Fourth of July was always my favorite holiday. We'd spend it out at my grandma's farm and head over to the tribal reservations to buy fireworks to set off as soon as the dusky sky turned dark. Berry shortcakes were a must for dessert—berries grew like weeds around the farm, and the shortcakes were so simple to make (and, of course, had those red, white, and blue colors for the holiday). I don't sweeten the coconut cream because the fruit itself tends to be quite sweet, but if you want to whisk in a teaspoon of agave or sugar, go right ahead. You can easily double or triple this recipe for a crowd: vegan or not, it's always a big hit. And really, the worst-case scenario is you'll have leftover berries to use in your morning yogurt or oatmeal, and biscuits to toast with some butter.

½ pound fresh blueberries

1 cup sugar

½ cup freshly squeezed lemon juice

½ pound fresh strawberries

1 (15-ounce) can coconut cream, chilled in the fridge overnight, then placed in the freezer 20 minutes before using (see page 7)

2 tablespoons coconut cream powder (see Chef's Note)

2 vanilla beans, sliced down the middle, seeds scraped out and reserved, pod discarded

4 Genesee Biscuits (page 201), sliced in half

1. Place a large mixing bowl in the freezer.

2. In a saucepan over medium-low heat, combine the blueberries, ½ cup of the sugar, and ¼ cup of the lemon juice. Cook, stirring occasionally, for 15 minutes. Remove from the heat and chill in the fridge. Repeat the process with the strawberries, the remaining ½ cup of sugar, and the remaining ¼ cup of lemon juice.

3. Remove the mixing bowl from the freezer and place the coconut cream, coconut cream powder, and seeds from the vanilla bean in the bowl, whisking by hand until fully combined. Using an electric mixer, whip on high speed for 4 to 5 minutes, until the cream has a little more than doubled in size. Using the whisk, dip it and pull up, and the mixture should come to a soft peak; if not, mix for an additional minute and test again. When finished, transfer the mixture to a cold serving bowl.

4. Place the sliced biscuits on a platter or large serving plate and serve with the berries and cream. Allow your guests to assemble their own shortcakes.

CHEF'S NOTE: *Coconut cream powder is dried coconut cream, and can be found at most Asian grocery stores. I add a little to the coconut cream to give it more lift and to help it hold its shape longer, but if you can't find it, just leave it out and whip up your coconut cream right before serving it. Frozen berries can be substituted when fresh ones are not available or in season.*

DEEP CHOCOLATE RASPBERRY CAKE, PAGE 208

DEEP CHOCOLATE RASPBERRY CAKE

AT THE CO-OP WHERE I USED to work, we made a ton of vegan chocolate cake using vinegar and baking soda as a leavening instead of eggs—and vegan or not, it was crazy delicious. Later I learned the technique was actually rooted in Depression-era cooking, from days when eggs were scarce and home cooks had to get infinitely creative in the kitchen. Years after my co-op stint, I've adapted this cake to include a little cayenne and cinnamon, and toasty Marcona almonds scattered on top for crunch. I'm not one for fussy desserts, so I like to assemble it right at the table in individual servings: one slice of cake, a spoonful of not-too-sweet raspberry topping, and a generous dollop of fluffy coconut icing. And we're in business.

¼ cup Marcona almonds, chopped

CAKE

½ cup unsweetened cocoa powder

2 cups all-purpose flour, plus more for dusting

1½ cups granulated sugar

2 teaspoons baking soda

½ teaspoon cayenne pepper

1 teaspoon ground cinnamon

½ teaspoon sea salt

1⅓ cups water

½ cup safflower oil

2 tablespoons red wine vinegar

Safflower or canola oil spray

RASPBERRY TOPPING

½ pound raspberries

½ cup granulated sugar

¼ cup freshly squeezed lemon juice

½ ounce Grand Marnier

FROSTING

1 vanilla bean, sliced down the middle, seeds scraped out and reserved, pod discarded

½ cup palm oil shortening

½ cup vegan butter

1½ cups powdered sugar

½ cup coconut cream, chilled in the fridge overnight (see page 7)

1. Preheat the oven to 350°F.

2. Place the almonds on a sheet pan or in a baking dish, and toast in the oven for 5 minutes, or until the nuts begin to lightly brown. Transfer to a plate and set aside.

3. In a large mixing bowl, sift together the cocoa powder, flour, granulated sugar, baking soda, cayenne, cinnamon, and salt. In a separate bowl, combine the water, oil, and vinegar. Add the wet ingredients to the dry and whisk together to combine. The mixture should be smooth.

4. Spray an 8-inch square cake pan with oil and dust with a small amount of flour. Pour the batter into the prepared pan and bake for 25 minutes, or until a toothpick comes out clean when inserted into the middle of the cake. Remove the cake from the oven and allow to cool in the pan.

5. In a saucepan over medium-low heat, combine the raspberry topping ingredients and simmer for 10 minutes. Transfer to a bowl and allow to cool in the fridge.

6. In a large mixing bowl or a stand mixer fitted with the whisk attachment, combine the vanilla bean, palm oil, and butter. Whip on medium speed, using an electric mixer or the stand mixer, for 5 to 6 minutes. You should start to see the mixture growing in volume. At this point, increase the speed to high, and the mixture should reach the point where it has doubled in size. At this point, sift the powdered sugar into the bowl, and slowly return the mixer to high speed. When the mixture is fully combined, slowly add the coconut cream, and mix on high speed for another 2 to 3 minutes.

7. When the cake is cool, cut it into squares and top each piece with some of the coconut frosting, then the raspberry topping, and finally the toasted almonds.

CHEF'S NOTE: *If you'd like to make cupcakes instead, scoop the batter into lined cupcake papers and adjust the baking time (cupcakes generally take 15 to 20 minutes' less time). Check frequently to avoid overbaking.*

METRIC CONVERSION CHARTS

The recipes in this book have not been tested with metric measurements, so some variations might occur. Remember that the weight of dry ingredients varies according to the volume or density factor: 1 cup of flour weighs far less than 1 cup of sugar, and 1 tablespoon doesn't necessarily hold 3 teaspoons.

OVEN TEMPERATURE EQUIVALENTS, FAHRENHEIT (F) AND CELSIUS (C)

100°F	= 38°C
200°F	= 95°C
250°F	= 120°C
300°F	= 150°C
350°F	= 180°C
400°F	= 205°C
450°F	= 230°C

GENERAL FORMULA FOR METRIC CONVERSION

Ounces to grams: Multiply ounces by 28.35

Grams to ounces: Multiply grams by 0.035

Pounds to grams: Multiply pounds by 453.5

Pounds to kilograms: Multiply pounds by 0.45

Cups to liters: Multiply cups by 0.24

Fahrenheit to Celsius: Subtract 32 from Fahrenheit temperature, multiply by 5, divide by 9

Celsius to Fahrenheit: Multiply Celsius temperature by 9, divide by 5, add 32

VOLUME (DRY) MEASUREMENTS

¼ teaspoon	= 1 milliliter
½ teaspoon	= 2 milliliters
¾ teaspoon	= 4 milliliters
1 teaspoon	= 5 milliliters
1 tablespoon	= 15 milliliters
¼ cup	= 59 milliliters
⅓ cup	= 79 milliliters
½ cup	= 118 milliliters
⅔ cup	= 158 milliliters
¾ cup	= 177 milliliters
1 cup	= 225 milliliters
4 cups or 1 quart	= 1 liter
½ gallon	= 2 liters
1 gallon	= 4 liters

VOLUME (LIQUID) MEASUREMENTS

1 teaspoon	= ⅙ fluid ounce	= 5 milliliters
1 tablespoon	= ½ fluid ounce	= 15 milliliters
2 tablespoons	= 1 fluid ounce	= 30 milliliters
¼ cup	= 2 fluid ounces	= 60 milliliters
⅓ cup	= 2⅔ fluid ounces	= 79 milliliters
½ cup	= 4 fluid ounces	= 118 milliliters
1 cup or ½ pint	= 8 fluid ounces	= 250 milliliters
2 cups or 1 pint	= 16 fluid ounces	= 500 milliliters
4 cups or 1 quart	= 32 fluid ounces	= 1,000 milliliters
1 gallon	= 4 liters	

WEIGHT (MASS) MEASUREMENTS

1 ounce	= 30 grams	
2 ounces	= 55 grams	
3 ounces	= 85 grams	
4 ounces	= ¼ pound	= 125 grams
8 ounces	= ½ pound	= 240 grams
12 ounces	= ¾ pound	= 375 grams
16 ounces	= 1 pound	= 454 grams

LINEAR MEASUREMENTS

½ inch	= 1½ cm
1 inch	= 2½ cm
6 inches	= 15 cm
8 inches	= 20 cm
10 inches	= 25 cm
12 inches	= 30 cm
20 inches	= 50 cm

SOURCES

While most of my produce comes from the farmers' market, one of our smaller neighborhood markets, or the Asian grocery, a few online retailers are superhelpful in sourcing more difficult-to-find ingredients or—to be honest—just convenient means of picking up supplies when life gets busy, as it's known to do. Here are a few of my favorites.

BOB'S RED MILL

www.bobsredmill.com

Bob's Red Mill sells a wide variety of whole grains, whole-grain flours, and nut flours and I rely on its vital wheat gluten and garbanzo bean flour for many of the core recipes in this book.

WORLD SPICE

www.worldspice.com

Despite the fact that many grocery stores in Seattle have a large bulk spice selection, some spices are still tough to find. For more obscure blends, such as the berbere spice for our Berbere Roasted Roots (page 139), I hit up World Spice.

PENZEY'S SPICE

www.penzeys.com

A great, general spice retailer, Penzey's selection is vast, so it always seems to have exactly what I'm looking for.

NEW ENGLAND CHEESEMAKING SUPPLY COMPANY

www.cheesemaking.com

To source a few pieces of cheesecloth, I find that these guys are always reasonably priced and well stocked.

LEM PRODUCTS

www.lemproducts.com

LEM Products is my go-to source for vegan sausage casings suitable for home use.

SPECTRUM ORGANICS

www.spectrumorganics.com

I rely on safflower oil and coconut oil for the recipes in this book and the cooking I do at home. Spectrum is a great online spot for organic, unrefined oils.

ASIAN FOOD GROCER AND KOA MART

www.asianfoodgrocer.com
www.koamart.com

In Seattle, I love shopping at Uwajimaya for Asian ingredients and produce, but if you're looking for a good online resource, Asian Food Grocer has a great selection of sauces and seasonings and KOA Mart specializes in more specialized Korean ingredients.

ACKNOWLEDGMENTS

While this book is a culmination of countless experiences and influences, it wouldn't be right unless I called out a few of them. To G, thanks for showing me how to work hard, have fun, and be myself. To my mom, dad, and sisters, for doing the dishes. To brown bread, garlic and mustard sandwiches, fosters, and following too close.

To the people that helped make this book happen, I am so grateful for your time and energy. Lacey McGarry, thank you for the late hours, reminders, organization, and for bringing it all together. To David Lee, for showing me that an idea will only be as good as the hard work you put behind it, for giving me a chance to grow and blossom, always challenging me to be better, and sharing your amazing family. To Sarah Flotard, Megan Gordon, and Blake Katagiri, your talents have been indispensable. To Bryanna Clark Grogan for being at the beginning. To our publishers and editors, specifically John Radziewicz for stumbling into the office one day and entertaining our ambitious undertaking, and Renée Sedliar for encouraging our progress and tirelessly poring through our drafts. Also to Alex Camlin, Miriam Riad, Kevin Hanover, Christine Marra, Iris Bass, and Lisa Diercks. To my friends Nate, Dyb, Ben, Simon, Liz, Ken, Bloxom and Lank, Nick, and all the adventures.

And to Liv and Eddy, I'm so lucky to be on your team.

INDEX

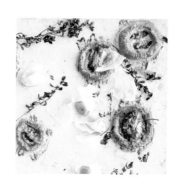